## CLASSIC COCKTAILS AND FANCY DRINKS WITH ANGOSTURA® BITTERS

# CLASSIC COCKTAILS AND FANCY DRINKS

WITH

# CONTENTS

# 200 YEARS OF ANGOSTURA® BITTERS

While it's now known as an essential ingredient for any cocktail lover, the first batch of our bitters was made by a doctor to relieve his patients' digestive and stomach disorders. The special tonic was developed in 1824 by Dr Johann Gottlieb Benjamin Siegert, the surgeon general in Simon Bolivar's revolutionary army in Venezuela. Originally named *Amargo Aromatico*, or 'Aromatic Bitters', it proved particularly popular with visiting sailors looking to quell their seasickness. It wasn't long before these sailors discovered that adding a dash or two of bitters to their ration of gin enhanced the flavour, creating one of the first Angostura cocktails – the Pink Gin – in the process.

In 1830, the tonic, now known as Dr Siegert's aromatic bitters, was exported for the first time to Trinidad and to England. The bitters later became known as Angostura® aromatic bitters, taking its name from the town where it was first created, Angostura in Venezuela, which is today known as Ciudad Bolívar. Dr Siegert continued to practise medicine for another 20 years before resigning to devote his full attention to the commercial development of his bitters.

In 1875, Dr Siegert's sons left Venezuela in possession of the secret formula for the bitters. They started production in Port of Spain, Trinidad, later setting up a rum distillery in Laventille in Trinidad and Tobago in 1949. The bitters has been produced here ever since and is still made to exactly the same recipe Dr Siegert first created 200 years ago.

Even though it's made on a small island, Angostura® bitters has been renowned across the world since its creation and picked up a number of prestigious awards in London, Paris and Vienna in the nineteenth century. By the early twentieth century, Angostura was appointed as purveyor to a number of royal households in Europe, including Wilhelm II – the King of Prussia, King Alfonso XIII of Spain and King George V of Great Britain. In 1955, the company received a royal warrant from Queen Elizabeth II, who later visited the distillery in Trinidad and Tobago.

While there have been many twists and turns over the past 200 years, with the Trinidadian government even having to step in twice to keep production in Trinidad and Tobago, it has been a golden age of cocktails that has helped establish the bitters for centuries to come. One of the first recorded definitions of a cocktail, from a local paper in New York in 1806, calls it 'a stimulating liquor, composed of spirits of any kind, sugar, water and bitters'. Since then, bitters has become an essential ingredient in some of our favourite cocktails. Without it, the Old Fashioned, Manhattan and Champagne Cocktail simply would not exist today. In Harry Craddock's seminal work, *The Savoy Cocktail Book*, first published in 1930, over 90 recipes mentioned Angostura® bitters specifically by name.

Over the last 200 years, Angostura has never stopped innovating. From the creation of an award-winning rum portfolio, an amaro and line of bitter-based refreshers, to the creation of orange bitters in 2007 and cocoa bitters in 2020, the company has always been on top of what's trending in the cocktail world. Its commitment to quality means Angostura® bitters has stood the test of time and is as revered today as it was when it was first created 200 years ago.

# A JEWEL OF
# TRINIDAD AND TOBAGO

Today Angostura is one of Trinidad and Tobago's crown jewels, and its two centuries of history is a testament to the company's ambitious thinking and diverse cultural influences.

Trinidad and Tobago has the incredible white sandy beaches, crystal clear turquoise waters and windswept palm trees we've come to expect from the Caribbean, as well as the most exquisite Hindu temples and a vibrant food and music scene. As a historically important commercial transit port, Trinidad has become an industrialised, metropolitan island, with a diverse mixture of vibrant cultures, which can be seen in everything from its distinctive food and drink to music and art.

Trinidad is blessed with an abundance of flora and fauna, including more than 100 species of butterflies and 18 species of hummingbird. Incredible botanicals, bountiful ingredients and an appreciation for diverse flavours influence a vibrant food and drink scene on the island.

Culturally, Trinidadians are very creative people. Everything on the island has a sense of theatre, from swizzling a cocktail to dancing in the streets on Carnival Monday and Tuesday. Trinidad Carnival is world famous and the energy that flows through the streets cannot be replicated anywhere else.

The techniques and knowledge of distilling in Trinidad came from the Portuguese Fernandes family. One of the first blenders and distillers on the islands, the Fernandes distillery was later acquired by and merged with Angostura. The style of rum produced by Angostura in Trinidad and Tobago reflects a diverse culture, with influences from the British, Spanish, Portuguese and French.

There is a palpable pride from Trinidadians at the global success of Angostura. It really means something that they can find that distinctive oversized label and yellow cap behind just about any bar in the world and know it came from home.

# A STORY
# IN EVERY DASH

**THAT LABEL!**

With its oversized label and bright yellow cap, a bottle of our bitters is instantly recognisable. But did you know that this iconic look was the product of a tight deadline? Two of the Siegert brothers were entering their father's recipe into a number of international competitions and one was in charge of creating the bottle while the other worked on the label. When the two came together, they discovered that their creations didn't quite fit together. It's unknown whether the bottle was too small or the label was too big, but the brothers had run out of time, so the bottle was entered as it was.

While the creation of the oversized label was a happy accident, the decision to stick with it for all these years was a stroke of marketing genius.

**THE SECRET TO SUCCESS**

Angostura's success is in part due to its ability to keep a secret. The botanicals in the bitters are weighed out in a secret room within the distillery. Only five people are privy to that specific recipe and none of them know who the others are. Each of these manufacturers measures their individual portion inside that room, alone and away from prying eyes.

The Trinidadian government also assists in keeping the recipe secret. The botanicals are imported into Trinidad and Tobago using a coded number system. It's even written into law that no government official can ask for or disclose the contents of the botanicals being imported for the production of the bitters. It no longer takes a family, but a whole island, to keep Angostura's recipe a secret.

## THE MEDALS

The medals that grace the label of each and every bottle of the bitters are both sides of the Medal of Excellence that Angostura was awarded at the Grand Exhibition in Vienna in 1873. These medals, combined with the signature of Dr JGB Siegert, make up the bitters' trademark and act as a warning to potential imitators.

## BY ROYAL APPOINTMENT

Angostura is the first and only Caribbean company to hold a royal warrant. In 1955, Queen Elizabeth II awarded Angostura® bitters its royal warrant and, 30 years later, she personally visited the House of Angostura in Trinidad and Tobago.

## SURPRISING ALTERNATIVE USES FOR BITTERS

Our bitters is known as both a culinary and cocktail ingredient, but there are also some rather surprising other uses for the bitters. Canon Bar in Seattle used copious amounts of bitters to stain its bar a deep mahogany colour. In the Caribbean, rubbing bitters on your skin is said to make an excellent mosquito repellent. It will likely also stain your skin, so it's maybe not the go-to option!

# STYLES OF DRINKS

Bitters became synonymous with cocktails from the very beginning, helping to perfect flavourful drinks that stimulate the senses.

A great cocktail must be balanced and pleasing to the palate, nose and eye. An outstanding cocktail is a full sensory experience. Balance in cocktails is all about proportions – finding the perfect place between tart and sweet, strong and weak to create a drink which is more than the sum of its parts, where no single element overshadows or outshines any other.

Bitters is a pro tool to help bring drinks into balance. Our bitters can bind together ingredients and balance them out, all while adding a rich, complex depth of flavour. There are a number of different cocktail styles outlined in this book, which have stood the test of time and spawned countless variations. Understanding the basic principles behind each style can help you be more creative in your cocktail experiments.

## HIGHBALL

As well as being the name of a tall glass, a highball is a long, refreshing drink that includes a spirit and a carbonated mixer. Whisky and soda has become synonymous as the default choice for a highball and can be a delicious aperitif. Ice is the unspoken ingredient here – the more you have, the colder and more delicious the highball, so pack the glass high. The trick to a good highball is to not over-stir, lest you agitate the bubbles too much and lose the effervescence of the drink. Refrigerate your soda if you can before pouring, as colder soda retains more bubbles.

## MARTINI

The martini is the original king of cocktails and is quite literally an icon. In the first edition of Harry Cradock's *The Savoy Cocktail Book*, a classic martini called for equal measures of gin, French vermouth and a dash of orange bitters. Today, the Fifty Fifty Martini is back in fashion in some quarters, but a dry martini will typically call for a ratio of between 3:1 and 5:1 gin to dry vermouth. The craft cocktail revival of the early 2000s saw the dry martini with orange bitters take centre stage once more due to that zesty lift.

## SOUR

A sour is a very old and broad style of cocktail that includes a spirit, citrus and sweetener, often with bitters and egg white. The classic ratio for a sour is two parts spirit, one part citrus and half a part sugar. A sour will always be shaken, never stirred, in order to fully integrate the citrus and egg white. Sours have that perfect balance of tart and sweet, and a beautiful velvety texture and mouthfeel.

## SLING

Slings first became popular towards the end of the eighteenth century, pre-dating other types of cocktail. At its simplest, a sling is a mix of spirit, sugar and water. The most famous type is the Singapore Sling, which includes spirits, citrus, liqueurs and other sweeteners.

## SWIZZLE

A swizzle is a style of drink defined less by the ingredients than the motion required to make it. Typically, this is a rum-based drink with citrus (usually lime), sweetener and bitters. To make the drink, take a swizzle stick between the palms of both hands and rub them back and forth quickly. The swizzle stick was first created from the branch of a tree native to the Caribbean that has little prongs at the end that act as a whisk and churn up ice in crushed ice drinks.

# COCKTAIL KIT

There are a few key pieces of equipment you need to make drinks with the bitters. While you can always get more fancy as you go, here are the basics you'll need to start mixing fancy drinks.

### SHAKER

If you invest in one thing, a good shaker is an essential part of any kit. They're not super expensive and will certainly help raise your cocktail game. A three-piece shaker is great for mixing individual drinks and a two-piece Boston shaker can be easier when making multiple servings. Either works well.

### MIXING GLASS

Having a mixing glass on hand for stirred drinks such as martinis is ideal. But if you don't have one to hand, you can use the glass of a cafetière. If using an alternative, the glass may be a little thinner so take care, or simply stir in one part of a cocktail shaker.

### JIGGER

Getting the proportions right is the key to consistently good drinks and measuring out your spirits in a jigger is a pro move. Hourglass-shaped jiggers with two different measures on each end are widely available and aren't that expensive. However, if you don't have a jigger to hand, you can use a shot glass or egg cup to measure liquids.

## SWIZZLE STICK

You can't make a swizzle without a swizzle stick, which comes from the branches of the *Quararibea turbinata*, a tree native to the Caribbean, where the tradition of swizzling stems from. This is one tool we recommend that you order, as it'll add some nice theatre to your drink-making and be a great talking point while you're entertaining.

## BAR SPOON

A long, metal bar spoon is necessary for stirring drinks to perfection. It can also double up as a measuring tool – a bar spoon holds 5ml of liquid.

## STRAINER

A strainer is the best way to ensure your drinks are both delicious to drink and pleasing to look at.
A Hawthorne strainer will ensure solid ingredients like fruit or herbs don't make their way into the drink, while a fine strainer will stop even small shards of ice from passing through and is ideal when you want a crystal clear drink.

## MUDDLER

A muddler is a sturdy tool to bruise and bash ingredients to release the juices and oils. If you don't have one to hand, use the end of a rolling pin or something wooden with a broad, round base.

# GLASSES

The choice of glassware adds to a drink and its visual appeal, so fancy glassware helps make fancy drinks. Most of the cocktails in this book can be made using just the first three styles of glass, but if you want to invest in more here's a little overview.

### HIGHBALL
A tall glass that's ideal for serving mixed drinks with plenty of ice.

### ROCKS GLASS
This is a short, sturdy, wide-rimmed glass with a strong base that traditionally took a beating when sugar was being pummelled to make an Old Fashioned.

### COUPE
A coupe is a Champagne saucer with a long stem and shallow bowl and is a classic choice for fancy drinks served without ice. The coupe's wide rim makes for easy sipping with an elegant touch. You should only hold the glass by the stem, not the bowl, even when serving, so as not to warm the icy cold drink inside.

### MARTINI
This is a classic cocktail glass that's similar to a coupe, but usually has straight angular sides.

### CHAMPAGNE FLUTE

A Champagne flute is another stemmed glass but with a tall slender shape and narrower rim to preserve more of the bubbles from Champagne. This flute glass helps to elevate any occasion and screams sophistication. A coupe can also serve as a substitute for this glass as needed.

### NICK & NORA

A stemmed glass with a higher-sided bowl, which means it can hold more liquid with less risk of spilling during bustling parties – a fact that has made it a favourite in bars and home bars alike. Save your carpets and get a few of these for dinner parties.

### OTHER SPECIALITY GLASSES

There are many other speciality glasses that look superb and make a statement. A Hurricane glass is curvaceous, with a flared rim that showcases the aromatics of tropical drinks wonderfully and leaves plenty of space for creative garnishes. The Pearl Diver glass is perfect for tiki-style drinks, while the bulbous Brandy Snifter was originally designed to capture the delicate aromatics of a cognac but can work equally well for cocktails. A Cordial glass is short-stemmed and is perfect for a small, neat aperitif.

# THE ANGOSTURA® BITTERS LINEUP

You are no doubt familiar with Angostura® aromatic bitters, which has been helping to make drinks more delicious for 200 years and is easily identifiable by that iconic oversized label and yellow cap.

But are you familiar with the rest of the range, developed with the deep-rooted expertise in botanicals and bitters mixed with a little creative flair?

## ANGOSTURA®
## AROMATIC BITTERS

Angostura is the gold standard in bitters – its quality, consistency and ability to bind, balance, enhance and elevate drinks is unparalleled.

Bartenders all over the world use the bitters to elevate their cocktails, where it works particularly well with aged spirits like whisky, bourbon, rum and pisco. As many drinks lovers will know, it's the essential ingredient in a Manhattan and an Old Fashioned. It's often been called the salt and pepper of the bar world for its ability to enhance a drink and marry flavours together. While you may not notice the bitters in your drink, you'll surely notice its absence.

## ANGOSTURA®
## ORANGE BITTERS

The award-winning orange bitters enlivens cocktails with a deep citrus burst of brightness, which amplifies and infuses drinks with unrivalled layers of orange flavour and warming notes of aromatic spices to finish. It works well with white spirits, such as rum, gin, tequila and vodka, where it brightens cocktails, elegantly accentuating the citrus tang in a Martini, Margarita or a Daiquiri.

The orange bitters is crafted by combining citrus essences from both sun-ripened bitter and lusciously sweet oranges, harmoniously balanced by a rich medley of herbs and spices.

## ANGOSTURA®
## COCOA BITTERS

The cocoa bitters is a celebration of Angostura's provenance as it contains nibs of Trinidad and Tobago's agricultural gem, the indigenous Trinitario cocoa. Trinitario is one of the world's finest hybrid cocoas and was developed in Trinidad and Tobago more than 250 years ago. Trinitario is highly valued by chocolatiers all over the world for its distinctive, bold, fruity and often floral flavour. The bitters uses the nibs to provide top notes of rich, floral, nutty cocoa, combining them with an intoxicating infusion of aromatic botanicals.

The cocoa bitters pairs perfectly with sweet vermouth or aged spirits, such as whiskey, rum, cognac and tequila. It works incredibly well in coffee drinks, such as the classic Espresso Martini (page 174) and the Café Trinidad (page 184).

### ANGOSTURA®
### 200-YEAR ANNIVERSARY
### LIMITED EDITION BITTERS

To mark its 200-year anniversary, Angostura unveiled a limited edition commemorative blend of bitters that pays tribute to two centuries of unparalleled craftsmanship and flavour mastery. This bitters stands out for its distinctive blend of premium botanicals such as aged rum, Angelica root, Roman wormwood, and nutmeg. Unlike standard bitters, it offers a luxurious flavor profile with nuanced notes of cardamom, orange, and earthy undertones, creating an elevated and unique taste experience.

A key botanical ingredient in many traditional bitters recipes, Roman wormwood adds complexity and depth to the blend, while angelica root provides herbal, earthy and slightly sweet notes. With a limited batch of 120,000 bottles, why not use this unique ingredient in one of two celebratory cocktails and savour a bitters that is truly special?

# CLASSIQUE

Rich, elegant and opulent

This simple yet sophisticated cocktail celebrates four iconic leaders of their category. The base of this drink is Angostura® 1824 rum, so named after the year the bitters was first created. This elegant drink is elevated by Lillet Blanc vermouth, Champagne and the very special limited release Angostura® 200-year anniversary limited edition bitters.

### INGREDIENTS
- 50ml Angostura® 1824 rum
- 25ml Lillet Blanc vermouth
- 2 dashes of Angostura® 200-year anniversary limited edition bitters
- 30ml Champagne

### GARNISH
* 1 brandied cherry

### GLASS
* Elegant coupe, chilled

### METHOD
1. Add the rum, vermouth and bitters to a mixing glass.
2. Add ice and stir for 15 seconds until well chilled.
3. Strain into a chilled coupe.
4. Top with the Champagne and garnish with a brandied cherry.

# VIP PALOMA

Fresh, vibrant, fruity

The Paloma is the most popular tequila-based cocktail in Mexico; it's vibrantly refreshing and simultaneously sweet, sour and bitter. This VIP Paloma is elevated by the addition of Angostura® 200-year anniversary limited edition bitters and prosecco. It's a bubbly beauty of a drink.

### INGREDIENTS

- 45ml 100% agave reposado tequila
- 90ml grapefruit soda
- 2 dashes of Angostura® 200-year anniversary limited edition bitters
- Prosecco, to top

### GARNISH

* Grapefruit wedge and a sprig of fresh rosemary

### GLASS

* Highball

### METHOD

1. Add the tequila to a highball glass filled with ice.
2. Add the grapefruit soda and bitters and stir gently.
3. Top with prosecco.
4. Garnish with a grapefruit wedge and a sprig of rosemary.

In the modern age, mixology has surpassed its traditional boundaries and made its mark in unexpected places. Whether you're concocting a quick mixer for a cosy date night, crafting an impressive libation to dazzle friends, or even opting for a sophisticated creation sans liquor, the concept of a 'cocktail' has evolved to take on various definitions.

Although it may appear complex, the world of mixology offers a rich canvas of recipes to inspire your inner bartender. From seasoned mixologists to eager beginners, this collection of recipes encourages everyone to explore and experiment. Each recipe celebrates the artistry and versatility of classic mixology, inviting you to craft drinks for any occasion with a flair and finesse that is uniquely yours.

# PART 1

★

# THREE-INGREDIENT CLASSICS

Three is the magic number. This chapter proves
drinks don't need to be complicated to be delicious.
When there are fewer ingredients, the proportions
and careful balance of how the drink is put together
becomes even more important.

You'll find two of the three best loved classic
cocktails in this chapter – the Old Fashioned
and Manhattan.

# A STORY IN EVERY DASH:
# THE OLD FASHIONED

Evolved from the Whiskey Cocktail, the Old Fashioned was first referenced in 1888 in *The Bartender Manual* by Theodore Proulx and predates both the Martini and the Manhattan.

It's one of only a few drinks that spawned the name of a glass used to make it, being built in a heavy-bottomed squat glass often referred to as an Old Fashioned glass. According to the original recipe, a sugar cube soaked in the bitters was muddled into a paste with a bar spoon of warm water before whiskey and ice were added, which meant the glass would need to be pretty thick and sturdy to withstand the regular bashing.

Nowadays, simple syrup is often used in place of a sugar cube to speed up the creation of this drink somewhat, but it still takes a little time to make, which is rewarded by the liquid in the glass.

The Old Fashioned survived Prohibition, which outlawed the production of its core ingredient, American whiskey, and came back stronger for it. By the 1940s and 1950s, it was almost an essential on every bar menu. Today, the Old Fashioned is still very much in fashion.

# OLD FASHIONED

Sweet, rich, spirit-forward

Beloved by whiskey fans the world over, the original whiskey cocktail has taken many forms and at one point veered into a fruity drink served long over ice. That's when old timers started to call for the 'Old Fashioned' whiskey cocktail they knew and loved. Over a century later, the name has stuck. It's the very definition of a cocktail – spirits, water, sugar and bitters – and is considered a national institution by many in the United States.

### INGREDIENTS
* 50ml bourbon or rye whiskey
* 5ml simple syrup
* 2 dashes of Angostura® aromatic bitters

### GARNISH
* Orange twist

### GLASS
* Rocks

### METHOD
1. Pour half of the whiskey into a rocks glass, add a couple of ice cubes and stir.
2. Add the simple syrup, bitters and a couple more ice cubes and stir some more.
3. Add the remaining whiskey and some more ice and, guess what, stir again.
4. Garnish with an orange twist.

*Some say rye whiskey is the traditional spirit here and using rye means the drink packs more of a punch and has a delicious, spicy kick. Others favour bourbon which leads to a mellower, softer Old Fashioned.*

# STONE FENCE

*Sweet, tart and spice*

This simplest of American highballs dates back to the Colonial era and was originally made with rum as the base. By 1862 Jerry Thomas's *Bartenders Guide* called for this drink with bourbon and, after Prohibition, Scotch became a popular base. It's a wonderfully flavourful autumnal drink that works with whatever dark spirit you happen to have at home.

### INGREDIENTS
- 60ml aged rum, brandy or bourbon/rye
- 1 dash of Angostura® aromatic bitters
- 150ml fresh apple juice

### GARNISH
* A sprig of fresh mint, a twist of lemon peel or freshly grated nutmeg

### GLASS
* Highball

### METHOD
1. Fill a highball glass with ice.
2. Add all the ingredients.
3. Stir gently.
4. Garnish with a mint sprig, a twist of lemon peel or freshly grated nutmeg.

---

*This is a versatile drink that you can adapt to whatever dark spirit you happen to have on hand. Opting for bourbon brings notes of vanilla and caramel, rye brings on a nice baking spice, rum provides a rich sweetness, and brandy brings additional fruity, oaky notes.*

# THE CHAMPAGNE COCKTAIL

Opulent, aromatic, sparkling

This is one of the simplest and classiest cocktails which appeared in the original *Bartenders Guide* in 1862. The base of this drink is a sugar cube soaked in bitters, which is then topped with Champagne. This drink is a treat for the senses. The Champagne slowly eats away at the sugar at the bottom, launching a persistent stream of fine bubbles while you sip.

### INGREDIENTS
- 1 sugar cube
- 4 dashes of Angostura® aromatic bitters
- Champagne, to top

### GARNISH
* Twist of lemon peel or a cherry

### GLASS
* Champagne flute

### METHOD
1. Place the sugar cube at the bottom of a Champagne flute.
2. Add the bitters until the sugar cube is soaked.
3. Fill the glass with Champagne and garnish with a lemon twist or a cherry.

*Add 10ml of cognac on top of the bitters-soaked sugar cube for an extra layer of flavour and complexity.*

# JAPANESE COCKTAIL

Rich, sweet nuttiness

A drink created by the celebrated bartender 'Professor' Jerry Thomas
in the mid-nineteenth century, the Japanese Cocktail is thought to
pay homage to one of Thomas's patrons, Tateishi Onojiro-Noriyuki.
He was an interpreter on Japan's first diplomatic mission to America
and seemed to have a ball at Thomas's bar. The rich fruity elegance
of the cognac combined with the sweet nuttiness of orgeat is balanced
by a couple of dashes of bitters.

### INGREDIENTS
- 60ml cognac
- 10ml orgeat syrup
- 2 dashes of Angostura® aromatic bitters

### GARNISH
* Twist of lemon peel

### GLASS
* Coupe, chilled

### METHOD
1. Add all the ingredients to a cocktail shaker.
2. Add ice and shake for around 30 seconds until well chilled.
3. Strain into a chilled coupe glass and garnish with a twist of lemon peel.

*Orgeat, pronounced* or-zhaat, *is an almond syrup that
adds a distinctive sweetness to drinks. It is a good amount
of work to make but thankfully very easy to buy these
days. It's also a key sweetener in many tiki-style drinks,
so worth having in a home bar.*

# MANHATTAN

*Elegant, bittersweet, spice*

The origins of the Manhattan may be disputed but, unlike the Martini, most agree on the classic proportions: two parts whiskey to one part sweet vermouth and a few dashes of bitters to balance and bind. This classic cocktail, first published in 1882, has never gone out of style. It's a combo that has become iconic and arguably one of the most riffed upon drinks.

### INGREDIENTS
- 60ml rye whiskey
- 30ml sweet vermouth
- 2 dashes of Angostura® aromatic bitters

### GARNISH
* Maraschino cherry

### GLASS
* Martini

### METHOD
1. Combine all the ingredients in a mixing glass.
2. Half-fill with ice and stir for around 20 seconds until well chilled.
3. Strain into a chilled martini glass.
4. Garnish with a maraschino cherry.

> *If you prefer Scotch to whiskey, switch out the rye for a Scottish single malt or blend and you have a Rob Roy.*

# STAR

Rounded, sweet elegance

A twist on a Manhattan that uses apple brandy instead of whiskey, the Star first found fame in the 1890s. Often made 'perfect' with equal parts apple brandy and sweet vermouth with a couple of dashes of bitters, our version uses a 2:1 ratio of apple brandy to sweet vermouth. The use of apple brandy in place of rye makes this an elegantly fruity, more approachable type of Manhattan.

### INGREDIENTS
- 60ml apple brandy
- 30ml sweet vermouth
- 2 dashes of Angostura® aromatic bitters

### GARNISH
* Maraschino cherry

### GLASS
* Coupe, chilled

### METHOD
1. Add all the ingredients to a mixing glass half-filled with ice.
2. Stir for 15–20 seconds until well chilled.
3. Strain into a chilled coupe glass.
4. Garnish with a maraschino cherry.

*We've dialled back the sweet vermouth here to adapt the original recipe for a modern palate but play around with the proportions to suit your tastes.*

# TUXEDO

Savoury, tangy, pungent

The Tuxedo cocktail dates back to the 1890s and takes its name, not from the dinner jacket, but a private members club called the Tuxedo Park. Fino sherry is bone dry and adds a nutty richness that is lifted by the citrus burst of orange bitters. At home at a black tie dinner, this stylish, savoury riff on a Martini has appeared in many esteemed cocktail books.

### INGREDIENTS
- 60ml gin
- 30ml fino sherry
- 2 dashes of Angostura® orange bitters

### GARNISH
* Orange twist

### GLASS
* Martini, chilled

### METHOD
1. Add all the ingredients to a chilled mixing glass.
2. Half-fill with ice and stir well for around 15–20 seconds.
3. Strain into a chilled martini glass.
4. Garnish with an orange twist.

> *Like most Martini riffs, there are many variations on a Tuxedo. Some recipes call for a dash or two of maraschino liqueur to add sweetness or absinthe for a herbal note. You can also play with the ratio of gin to fino, or opt for a richer style of sherry, such as an amontillado if you find the fino too dry.*

# ALASKA

Sweet, herbaceous, spirited

This variation on a Martini, which confusingly is not from Alaska, uses yellow chartreuse in place of vermouth for a hint of sweet herbs. Originally made with a sweet Old Tom gin, it's now made with a classic London dry gin, which is more readily available. This drink has enjoyed a cult following among cocktail enthusiasts since the early 1900s, as it provides a subtly sweet, herbaceous twist on a Martini.

### INGREDIENTS
- 60ml gin
- 15ml yellow chartreuse
- 3 dashes of Angostura® orange bitters

### GARNISH
* Lemon twist

### GLASS
* Coupe, chilled

### METHOD
1. Add all the ingredients to a mixing glass and half-fill with ice.
2. Stir for around 30 seconds until well chilled.
3. Strain into a chilled coupe glass and garnish with a lemon twist.

> *Much like a classic Martini, people's personal preferences with ratios vary wildly. If you like your drink a little sweeter, go harder on the yellow chartreuse. If you want to retain just a hint of that herbal sweetness, play with a 5:1 or 6:1 ratio of gin to yellow chartreuse.*

# RUM MANHATTAN

Rich, sweetness and spice

During Prohibition, it was much easier to get your hands on rum than rye whiskey, which had all but ceased production. The Rum Manhattan came into its own at this time as a twist on the classic cocktail which used rum in place of rye for a sweeter, rounder finish. The elegance of a Manhattan with the layered complexity and rich sweetness of a rum, combined with sweet vermouth and bitters make this a classic.

### INGREDIENTS
- 40ml Angostura® 1824 aged rum
- 20ml sweet vermouth
- 1 dash of Angostura® aromatic bitters

### GARNISH
* Maraschino cherry

### GLASS
* Coupe, chilled

### METHOD
1. Combine the rum, vermouth and bitters in a mixing glass.
2. Half-fill with ice and stir until the drink is well chilled – around 30 seconds.
3. Strain into a chilled coupe glass and garnish with a maraschino cherry.

*This is a recipe where the rum is allowed to shine and be the star of the show, so use a good-quality aged rum and allow the bitters to bind the flavours together.*

# THE BENNETT

Tangy, citrus, spice

The Bennett was featured in the 1922 cocktail book, *Cocktails: How to Mix Them* and was originally made with Old Tom gin, lime and a good few dashes of bitters. Modern iterations popularised by Meaghan Dorman at The Bennett in New York call for the more popular London dry gin. It's a refreshing gimlet and, with a couple of dashes of bitters, what's not to love?

### INGREDIENTS
- 60ml gin
- 45ml lime cordial
- 2 dashes of Angostura® aromatic bitters

### GARNISH
* Lime wheel

### GLASS
* Martini, chilled

### METHOD
1. Add all the ingredients to a cocktail shaker.
2. Half-fill with ice and shake for around 20 seconds.
3. Strain into a chilled martini glass and garnish with a lime wheel.

> *If you're being fancy, you can make your own lime cordial or use fresh lime juice and simple syrup.*

★

# DRINKS FOR SUNNY DAYS

Is there any better way to cool off on a hot, sunny day than with a crisp cocktail? This is a collection of classic cocktails and modern drinks that sing of sunshine.

While these sunny day cocktails are all great fun, they can also be serious and sophisticated drinks. The classic combination of rum, sugar, lime and bitters in a Daiquiri can be every bit as elegant as a Martini or a Manhattan. Beyond rum, there's a great whiskey twist on a Mai Tai, with a Rye Tai, a tequila-tiki drink with Doctor Limebender and a gin homage to summer and Snoop Dogg's classic 'Gin and Juice'.

# A STORY IN EVERY DASH:
# THE QUEEN'S PARK SWIZZLE

★

The Queen's Park Swizzle was the signature cocktail at the Queen's Park Hotel, a luxury tropical getaway in Trinidad and Tobago. In its 1920s heyday, it served sophisticated drinks to thirsty, well-heeled travellers.

A rum-based drink served over crushed ice, the Queen's Park Swizzle is a refreshing blend of sour and sweet, as pungent mint and freshly squeezed lime juice are balanced by demerara sugar and a generous quantity of bitters.

A swizzle is a style of drink that gets its name not from the ingredients or flavours but from the motion of making it – swizzling. To make one you need a swizzle stick, traditionally made from branches of the *Quararibea turbinata* tree, now known as the swizzle stick tree. The branches of the tree, native to the Caribbean, end in little fingers that act like a whisk, which help to churn crushed ice in a theatrical fashion.

# QUEEN'S PARK SWIZZLE

A vibrantly refreshing sipper

A classic swizzle from Trinidad and Tobago. Making this drink is a spectacle and piece of theatre in itself. It was first created at the Queen's Park Hotel, an upscale 1920s tropical retreat in the beating heart of Port of Spain. It's a drink with colour, vibrancy and a ton of flavour, encapsulating Trinidad perfectly. The crucial ingredient is, of course, Trinidad and Tobago's very own bitters.

### INGREDIENTS

- 12–14 fresh mint leaves
- 30ml fresh lime juice
- 30ml demerara simple syrup
- 60ml Angostura® 7 year old rum
- 6–8 dashes of Angostura® aromatic bitters

### GARNISH

* A sprig of fresh mint

### GLASS

* Highball

### METHOD

1. Build in a highball glass; muddle the mint leaves in the lime juice and simple syrup.
2. Fill the glass three-quarters full with dry crushed ice.
3. Pour the rum over the crushed ice and swizzle well until the glass is ice-cold and frosted.
4. Pack glass with more crushed ice and top with the bitters.
5. Garnish with a sprig of mint.

*It isn't a swizzle unless it is swizzled. To execute this West Indian cocktail technique, simply put the swizzle stick in the drink, place it between your palms and move them back and forth as quickly as you can.*

# SINGAPORE SLING

Tropical, lively, refreshing

The Singapore Sling is said to have been created at the Raffles Bar by a bartender named Ngiam Tong Boon. The cocktail at Raffles today is likely a lot sweeter and fruitier than the original style, which was said to be stronger with more herbal, citrus and spice. This twist on a Gin Sling was first created around the turn of the 20th century and, by the mid-1920s, the drink was known around the world.

### INGREDIENTS
- 45ml gin
- 45ml fresh pineapple juice
- 15ml Bénédictine liqueur
- 7.5ml Heering cherry liqueur
- 15ml fresh lime juice
- 7.5ml orange liqueur
- 1 dash of Angostura® aromatic bitters
- Chilled soda water, to top

### GARNISH
* Orange or pineapple slice and cherry

### GLASS
* Hurricane

### METHOD
1. Add all the ingredients, except the soda, into a shaker.
2. Add ice and shake for 10–15 seconds until well chilled and frothy.
3. Strain into a hurricane glass over fresh ice.
4. Top with chilled soda water.
5. Garnish with an orange slice or pineapple and cherry.

> It's been said that no two Singapore Sling recipes are quite alike. So why not play around with the proportions as you prefer? We've held back the pineapple here and ensured a good measure of gin for a Singapore Sling that is balanced and layered with a fruity, herbaceous bite.

# DAIQUIRI

Refreshingly zesty and tangy

This classic combination of rum, sugar, lime and bitters can be just as elegant as a Martini or Manhattan. Named after the harbour town of Daiquiri on Cuba's east coast, this drink was perfected by a couple of Havana bars during Prohibition. Bar La Florida was known as the Cathedral of the Daiquiri in the 1920s and it wasn't long before this drink was captivating revellers in US speakeasies.

### INGREDIENTS
- 60ml Angostura® 1919 rum
- 25ml fresh lime juice
- 15ml simple syrup
- 3 dashes of Angostura® aromatic bitters

### GARNISH
* Lime twist

### GLASS
* Coupe, chilled

### METHOD
1. Combine all the ingredients in a cocktail shaker.
2. Half-fill with ice and shake well for around 15 seconds.
3. Strain into a chilled coupe glass and garnish with a twist of lime.

*Skip a Strawberry Daiquiri, which can overpower the rum, and opt for a version named after the American writer Ernest Hemingway. This twist is frozen and uses 15ml of white grapefruit juice, a dash of maraschino cherry liqueur and the rest of the classic Daiquiri ingredients apart from the syrup. The result is a super tart, clean Daiquiri that is endlessly refreshing.*

# MAI TAI

Rich, zesty, sweet nuttiness

An iconic drink that came to define the tiki movement. The name is inspired by the Tahitian exclamation 'Mai tai roa ae!', which means 'Out of this world good!' Even though the original recipe was closely guarded by its creator, Trader Vic, so many rum lovers asked for this drink in other bars that mixologists were forced to figure out their own interpretations to meet consumer demand.

### INGREDIENTS

- 30ml Angostura® 5 year old gold rum
- 30ml Angostura® reserva white rum
- 30ml orange curaçao
- 15ml fresh lime juice
- 5ml orgeat syrup
- ½ teaspoon white cane sugar
- 2 dashes of Angostura® aromatic bitters

### GARNISH

* A sprig of fresh mint and a lime wedge

### GLASS

* Rocks

### METHOD

1. Add all the ingredients to a cocktail shaker.
2. Half-fill with ice and shake for around 15 seconds until well chilled.
3. Strain into an ice-filled rocks glass.
4. Garnish with a mint sprig and lime wedge.

> *The balance of sweet, sour and bitterness means the Mai Tai works really well with food – try it with island-inspired spiced marinated meats or zesty fresh seafood dishes.*

# OLD CUBAN

Decadent, crisp, lively

The Old Cuban is an elegant twist on a Mojito using a Champagne top that calls for an aged rum, hence the 'old'. Created in 2001 by the now legendary Audrey Saunders, it provided a glamorous signature to the landmark Bemelmans Bar at The Carlyle Hotel in New York. After it was debuted at The Ritz in London, the Old Cuban was celebrated in international press and started appearing on cocktail bar menus on both sides of the pond.

### INGREDIENTS
- 6 fresh mint leaves
- 20ml fresh lime juice
- 30ml simple syrup
- 45ml golden rum (we like Angostura® 1919 rum)
- 2 dashes of Angostura® aromatic bitters
- 60ml Champagne

### GARNISH
* A sprig of fresh mint

### GLASS
* Coupe

### METHOD
1. Muddle the mint leaves with the lime juice and sugar syrup in a cocktail shaker.
2. Add the rum, bitters and some ice and shake well for around 15 seconds until frothy.
3. Strain into a coupe glass and top with Champagne.
4. Garnish with a sprig of mint.

# FIVE ISLAND FIZZ

Citrus, gentle heat and fizz

The Five Island Fizz uses ingredients from five Caribbean islands: rum and bitters from Trinidad and Tobago, ginger beer from Barbuda, Jamaican limes and Velvet Falernum, a distinctive liqueur from Barbados. All ingredients are easily combined in the glass to provide a thirst-quenching, tangy drink with a warming sweet spice. A twist on a mule, the ginger beer lengthener provides refreshing bubbles with a little prickle of heat and spice that builds with each sip.

*David Delaney, USA, Angostura® Global Cocktail Challenge winner, 2012*

### INGREDIENTS

- 45ml Angostura® 5 year old rum
- 20ml Velvet Falernum
- 15ml fresh lime juice
- 2 dashes of Angostura® aromatic bitters
- 45ml Barritt's ginger beer
- 10ml Luxardo maraschino liqueur

### GARNISH

* Lime wheel, wrapped around a maraschino cherry

### GLASS

* Highball

### METHOD

1. Combine the rum, Velvet Falernum, lime juice and bitters in a highball glass.
2. Fill with crushed ice.
3. Top with the ginger beer.
4. Add the maraschino liqueur to provide the red top.
5. Garnish with a lime wheel wrapped around a maraschino cherry.

*Velvet Falernum is a Bajan classic liqueur used as a cocktail ingredient and is made with lime, almond, ginger, vanilla and clove. It can be a pain to make but is also easily available to buy.*

# RYE TAI

Tropical, soft, nutty sweetness

The Rye Tai packs a punch and is rounded out by pineapple juice for a refreshing tropical drink that whiskey lovers can enjoy on long summer days. Here, the nutty orgeat is balanced by tart lemon and the bitters top dances through the drink as you sip for a fun bit of visual theatre. It's a simple, fruity, whiskey-based tiki cocktail made with rye for an extra bite. If it's not yet a modern classic, it should be!

### INGREDIENTS
- 60ml rye whiskey
- 25ml fresh pineapple juice
- 25ml fresh lemon juice
- 25ml orgeat syrup
- 6–10 dashes of Angostura® aromatic bitters

### GARNISH
* A pineapple wedge

### GLASS
* Highball

### METHOD
1. Combine the whiskey, pineapple and lemon juices and orgeat in a cocktail shaker.
2. Half-fill with ice and shake well.
3. Strain into a highball glass with crushed ice.
4. Top with the bitters and garnish with a pineapple wedge.

*Pronounced or-zhaat, this almond syrup is a super pain to make, so just buy it as it's an essential part of tiki drinks that can't really be substituted.*

# DOCTOR LIMEBENDER

Hot, spice, fragrant

There's a tiki tradition of naming drinks after doctors, and this is our twist on the Doctor Mindbender, a devilishly good cocktail created by Death & Co's Matthew Belanger. It has the intense floral flavour of habanero chillies and the fruity sweetness of guava syrup in place of grenadine. It's a riff on a Mexican Firing Squad – a tart, refreshing classic – but our version turns up the heat with habanero infused tequila.

### INGREDIENTS
- 50ml Habanero infused tequila
- 20ml guava syrup
- 20ml fresh lime juice
- 2 dashes of Angostura® aromatic bitters

### GARNISH
* Lime wheel

### GLASS
* Hurricane

### METHOD
1. Add all the ingredients to a cocktail shaker.
2. Half-fill with ice and short shake for 10–15 seconds.
3. Strain into a Hurricane glass filled with cracked ice.
4. Garnish with a lime wheel.

---

*To make habanero tequila, take 3 habanero chilli peppers, remove the stems and seeds and cut into strips. Add to a bottle of your favourite blanco 100 per cent agave tequila. Leave it to rest at room temperature overnight and strain through a cheesecloth or sieve. Store in a cool dry place.*

# BUTTERFLY SWIZZLE

Tropical, tangy, aromatic

The swizzle is both a technique and a style of drink. To swizzle is a theatrical Caribbean bartending technique which uses a swizzle stick to mix together a crushed ice drink. This is a swizzle inspired by the butterflies that went into the sugar cane fields as a sign the sugarcane was ready to harvest. A swizzle is always a fancy drink, as it's made with such flair and theatre.

*Mike Jordhoy, Paris, Angostura® Global Cocktail Challenge finalist, 2020*

### INGREDIENTS

- 40ml Angostura® 7 year old rum
- 15ml banana liqueur
- 10ml fresh lime juice
- 10ml simple syrup
- 5ml amaro di Angostura®
- 4 dashes of absinthe
- 2 dashes of Angostura® orange bitters
- 5 dashes of Angostura® aromatic bitters

### GARNISH
* Flamed banana wedge

### GLASS
* Snifter

### METHOD

1. Build the drink in a snifter glass, except the bitters.
2. Add some dry crushed ice and swizzle.
3. Finish with more ice and the bitters.
4. Garnish with a wedge of flamed banana.

---

*To flame a banana, preheat a heavy-bottomed pan over a medium-high heat, toss in some butter, add sugar and stir until dissolved. Add banana slices then stir and flip until evenly coated and sizzle for 3–4 minutes. Carefully tilt the pan away from you and away from the flame and add a splash of rum. Jiggle the pan a little until it ignites. Once the flames die down, swirl the sauce in the pan a little more. If using an electric hob, hold a barbecue lighter near the pan to ignite.*

# SIPPIN' ON GIN AND JUICE

Tropical, tangy, fragrant

Named after the iconic 1994 Snoop Dogg track, Gin and Juice, this
pretty summer sipper is giving laid-back sunny days. A chilled mix of
hibiscus and rosehip-infused gin combined with a splash of pineapple,
lime, orgeat, triple sec and bitters for the win. Did you know it
was Snoop's mum who first introduced him to the joys of gin and
pineapple juice?

*Smoke & Bitters, Sri Lanka*

### INGREDIENTS
- 60ml hibiscus and rosehip-infused gin
- 15ml orgeat syrup
- 15ml triple sec
- 35ml fresh pineapple juice
- 17.5ml fresh lime juice
- 2 dashes of Angostura® aromatic bitters

### GARNISH
* Orange wheel, spiked with fresh cranberries and fresh rosemary

### GLASS
* Rocks

### METHOD
1. Combine all the ingredients in a cocktail shaker.
2. Add ice and shake for 15 seconds until well chilled.
3. Strain into a rocks glass with one big ice cube.
4. Garnish with an orange wheel spiked with cranberries and rosemary.

---

*To infuse gin with hibiscus and rose, place 30g dried hibiscus
and 30g dried rosehips in a 750ml bottle of gin and cold-infuse
in the fridge for 24 hours. Strain through a coffee filter.*

---

# SHAKEN
# NOT
# STIRRED

The rhythmic sound of a cocktail being shaken is the perfect
way to build anticipation for the drink that follows. It's a great
piece of theatre, but what is all that shaking actually doing?
It not only chills the drink and combines ingredients, but also
provides some aeration and texture to the liquid.

Many drinks using fruit juices or egg whites need to be shaken
for the ingredients to be properly combined. Included are two
sours – a New York Sour with an attractive red top and a Pisco
Sour with pretty bitters swirls on its frothy foam – as well as
classics, such as the Margarita, and underground favourites that
have become modern classics, like the London Calling.

# A STORY IN EVERY DASH:
# THE TRINIDAD SOUR

The Trinidad Sour is an unorthodox cocktail that upends convention by using bitters not to accentuate flavour, but as the core base of the drink itself. On paper, it doesn't look like it'll work and that is precisely why the drink has garnered such popularity – people, particularly bartenders, were curious as to what this would taste like.

Giuseppe González created the Trinidad Sour inspired by a drink made by fellow Italian Valentino Bolognese, the Trinidad Especial. After testing his recipe out on his bartender friends, the drink ended up being served as a bartender's special in Boston, San Francisco and London.

It's a cocktail that can be easily replicated with ingredients you'll find in any good cocktail bar – a hallmark of any modern classic. Ultimately, the cocktail's success is based on its unorthodox nature and memorability. The Trinidad Sour upsets the usual order of things, which makes it difficult to forget.

# TRINIDAD SOUR

Earthy, velvety, aromatic

Giuseppe González created this modern classic in 2009 while at the Clover Club in New York. Unusually, it uses bitters as the base 'spirit', which made it a standout cocktail that was soon replicated across the world. It's now classified as an IBA bartender classic cocktail and all pro bartenders are expected to know how to make it.

### INGREDIENTS
- 45ml Angostura® aromatic bitters
- 30ml orgeat syrup
- 25ml fresh lemon juice
- 10ml rye whiskey

### GLASS
* Coupe, chilled

### METHOD
1. Combine all the ingredients in a cocktail shaker.
2. Half-fill with ice and shake for 15 seconds until well chilled.
3. Strain into a chilled coupe glass.

> *Some bartenders choose to use egg white, a traditional sour ingredient, to give even more of a texture to this delicious drink.*

# NEW YORK SOUR

Silky, citrus, sour

Strangely enough, the New York Sour was not created in the US state but was likely later adopted and popularised by a bartender in the city. What makes a New York Sour unique is the distinctive red wine float. Egg white is also often added to the original recipe, which gives it a lovely velvety mouthfeel.

### INGREDIENTS
- 60ml bourbon
- 30ml fresh lemon juice
- 15ml simple syrup
- 1 egg white
- 3 dashes of Angostura® aromatic bitters
- 15ml red wine

### GARNISH
* Lemon twist

### GLASS
* Rocks

### METHOD
1. Add all the ingredients, except the red wine, to a cocktail shaker without ice and shake hard to whip up a foam.
2. Fill the shaker with ice and shake well for 20 seconds or so.
3. Fine strain into a rocks glass.
4. Fill the glass with ice, then top with a red wine float.
5. Garnish with a lemon twist.

> *Slowly pour the red wine over the back of a spoon to help the red wine float on the surface of the drink, just under the frothy egg white, creating the signature attractive red top.*

# CLOVER CLUB

*Zingy, bright, velvety*

The Clover Club was named after a drinking institution in Philadelphia frequented by a group of prominent reporters, which is possibly why this recipe was published as early as 1901. While it doesn't traditionally call for bitters, we think it adds a certain something to this drink. This sweet, tart pre-Prohibition drink was revived by Julie Reiner when she opened a bar in Brooklyn in 2008 bearing its name.

### INGREDIENTS
- 60ml London dry gin
- 30ml French dry vermouth
- 1 tsp raspberry syrup
- 1 egg white
- 15ml simple syrup
- ½ tsp lemon juice
- 3 dashes of Angostura® aromatic bitters

### GARNISH
* 3 fresh raspberries

### GLASS
* Wine

### METHOD
1. Combine all the ingredients, except the bitters, in a cocktail shaker.
2. Half-fill with ice and shake vigorously for around 20 seconds.
3. Strain into a small wine glass.
4. Add three dashes of the bitters on top.
5. Garnish with the fresh raspberries.

---

*If you don't have raspberry syrup, muddle a few raspberries at the bottom of the shaker, add a little extra rich simple syrup (2:1 sugar to water) and double strain.*

# PISCO SOUR

Light, zesty, aromatic

Pisco is an unoaked grape brandy that makes for a delicious sour. It was created by Victor Vaughen Morris, an American expat who went to Peru to work on the railroads and missed his whiskey sour. Today, a Pisco Sour is known for its zingy combination of pisco and lime shaken with egg white. The Pisco Sour is a classic cocktail from the 1920s and Peru's national drink. The Peruvian government celebrates the drink as a distinctive part of Peru's culture and heritage.

### INGREDIENTS
- 60ml pisco
- 25ml simple syrup
- 20ml fresh lime juice
- 1 egg white
- 8–10 dashes of Angostura® aromatic bitters

### GLASS
* Coupe, chilled

### METHOD
1. Add all the ingredients, except the bitters, to a cocktail shaker without any ice.
2. Shake for 20 seconds until all the ingredients are well mixed.
3. Add some ice and shake for a further 15 seconds until well chilled.
4. Strain into a chilled coupe glass.
5. Garnish with the bitters.

*Add the bitters to the foam top and use a cocktail stick to swirl it together to make pretty shapes.*

# THE LINE COCKTAIL

Rich, tangy sweetness

One of the earliest known classics to come out of Japan, The Line Cocktail combines equal parts gin, Bénédictine and sweet vermouth with a few dashes of bitters. Curiously for an all-spirit cocktail, which is typically stirred, The Line Cocktail is shaken – aerating the liquid and adding texture and body to this refreshing drink.

### INGREDIENTS
- 2 dashes of Angostura® aromatic bitters
- 10ml Bénédictine
- 10ml sweet vermouth
- 10ml dry gin

### GARNISH
* Crushed sweet pickled rakkyo (spring onion) or crushed pickled cocktail onion and a thin orange twist

### GLASS
* Cordial

### METHOD
1. Add all the ingredients to a cocktail shaker with just three cubes of ice.
2. Shake until very cold, around 15 seconds.
3. Strain into a cordial glass.
4. Garnish with crushed sweet pickled rakkyo (spring onion) or crushed pickled cocktail onion, if not available, and a thin twist of orange.

> *If you can't source sweet pickled rakkyo (spring onion), a pickled cocktail onion will do a similar job of adding the sweet and sour salinity that gives this drink a special flourish.*

# PEGU CLUB

Bright, bracing, citrus

The Pegu Club cocktail was the signature cocktail at the British officers' Pegu club in Yangon, Burma, now Myanmar. The judicious use of bitters adds complexity without overwhelming the drink, while the orange bitters helps to brighten the flavours. In 2005, it became the namesake of one of the most influential bars of the New York craft cocktail renaissance, Pegu Club, which sadly closed in 2020.

### INGREDIENTS
- 60ml gin
- 20ml fresh lime juice
- 20ml orange curaçao
- 2 dashes of Angostura® aromatic bitters
- 1 dash of Angostura® orange bitters

### GARNISH
* Lime wheel

### GLASS
* Coupe, chilled

### METHOD
1. Add all the ingredients to a cocktail shaker.
2. Add some ice and shake well for around 15 seconds.
3. Strain into a chilled coupe glass and garnish with a lime wheel.

# MARGARITA

Refreshing, citrus, bite

One of the earliest printed Margarita recipes is from Esquire, December 1953, which read, 'She's from Mexico, Señores, and her name is the Margarita Cocktail – and she is lovely to look at, exciting and provocative.' This simple combination of 100% agave tequila, orange liqueur and fresh lime juice can be elevated with a couple of dashes of orange bitters. There are several plausible but no proven origins of the Margarita cocktail, but what is undisputed is that the Margarita is currently one of the most popular cocktails in both the UK and US.

### INGREDIENTS
- Lime wedge and sea salt flakes, for the rim
- 50ml 100% agave blanco tequila
- 25ml triple sec orange liqueur
- 25ml fresh lime juice
- 2 dashes of Angostura® orange bitters

### GARNISH
* Lime wheel or twist

### GLASS
* Coupe

### METHOD
1. Half-rim the coupe glass with the lime wedge and sea salt flakes.
2. Combine the tequila, orange liqueur, lime juice and orange bitters in a cocktail shaker.
3. Half-fill with ice and shake until well chilled, around 15 seconds.
4. Fine strain into the chilled and salt-rimmed coupe glass.
5. Garnish with a lime wheel or twist.

---

*To half-rim a glass with salt, place a handful of sea salt flakes on to a plate. Slice a wedge of lime and make a small cut into its flesh. Squeeze the lime a little and run it along the side of the glass. Then, roll the glass rim in the sea salt. The lime juice will ensure it sticks.*

# LONDON CALLING

Nutty, dry, fruity

London Calling was one of the bestsellers at Milk & Honey, a Soho speakeasy on the London cocktail scene that sadly closed in 2020. It's a gin sour that uses fino sherry to provide distinctive salty, nutty notes that's lifted by the zesty orange bitters and grapefruit garnish. Named after punk band The Clash's seminal album, this drink has risen from the underground to international fame and is now considered a modern classic.

### INGREDIENTS
- 50ml gin
- 15ml fino sherry
- 15ml fresh lemon juice
- 10ml simple syrup
- 2 dashes of Angostura® orange bitters

### GARNISH
* Pink grapefruit twist

### GLASS
* Coupe, chilled

### METHOD
1. Add all the ingredients to a cocktail shaker.
2. Half-fill with ice and shake for around 15 seconds until well chilled.
3. Strain into a chilled coupe glass.
4. Garnish with a pink grapefruit twist.

*The original recipe called for a smaller measure of a higher proof navy-strength gin, so if you have some at hand give that a try. Some recipes call for equal measures of fino sherry, lemon juice and simple syrup, but we've dialled back the simple syrup here. However, you can play around with the proportions depending on your palate.*

# JULIET AND ROMEO

Fresh, floral, herbal

A refreshing summer cocktail that also sells particularly well on Valentine's Day. A Juliet and Romeo tastes like walking through an English garden – there's plenty of rose on the nose and on the palate there's a delicious mix of botanicals, lime, cucumber and mint. Created at one of Chicago's first craft cocktail bars in 2007, this one's a modern classic in the making.

### INGREDIENTS
- 3 slices of cucumber
- A pinch of salt
- 25ml simple syrup
- 60ml gin
- 25ml fresh lime juice
- A sprig of fresh mint
- 1 dash of rose water
- 3 dashes of Angostura® aromatic bitters

### GARNISH
* A fresh mint leaf

### GLASS
* Coupe, chilled

### METHOD
1. Add the cucumber and salt to a cocktail shaker and muddle.
2. Add the simple syrup, gin, lime juice and mint sprig to the shaker.
3. Half-fill with ice and shake for around 15 seconds until well chilled.
4. Strain into a chilled coupe glass.
5. Garnish with a mint leaf, add the dash of rose water on the mint leaf, then add the bitters.

*This is a crowd-pleaser of a cocktail – a gin cocktail for people who think they don't like gin – try it and win over some new friends! They'll be surprised in a good way.*

# JOHANN GOES TO MEXICO

Smoke, spice, citrus

The Johann Goes to Mexico is named after the creator of Angostura, Dr Johann Siegert. This mezcal drink is a memorable take on a Trinidad Sour, balancing the characteristic smoke of mezcal and the deep flavourful spice of bitters.

### INGREDIENTS
- 45ml mezcal, preferably Vida
- 15ml fresh lemon juice
- 15ml Angostura® aromatic bitters
- 15ml demerara syrup (see below)

### GLASS
* Cordial, chilled

### METHOD
1. Combine all the ingredients in a cocktail shaker.
2. Half-fill with ice and shake well for around 15 seconds.
3. Double strain into a chilled cordial glass.

> *To make a demerara syrup, combine equal measures of demerara sugar and water and heat gently in a pan until all the sugar is dissolved. Cool and strain into a sterilised glass bottle, refrigerate and use within a month.*

# SPIRITED DRINKS

When serving cocktails that are heavy on the liquor, with very little in the way of mixer, the quality of that base spirit is really important. These short drinks are designed for the spirit to shine. Generally, stronger drinks are stirred to chill and gently dilute without over-agitating by shaking, which can damage the delicate aromatics of the spirit.

We highlight a Martinez, a precursor to the Martini and often considered a Gin Manhattan, for its use of sweet vermouth in a gin drink. You'll also find some modern classics, like the Oaxaca Old Fashioned, one of the first cocktails to thrust mezcal on to the international scene and another good agave adaptation in the Rosita, a tequila twist on the Negroni. And if your preferred spirit base is rum or whiskey, we also have you covered with a honeyed Chet Baker or a twist on a Sazerac.

★

# A STORY IN EVERY DASH:
# THE MARTINI

★

First popularised in the 1890s, the Martini truly is the king of all cocktails. It has a cult-like following, transcending borders, generations and has infiltrated art, film and literature like no other drink.

Despite what James Bond would have you believe, the Martini is a stirred cocktail. The classic Dry Martini found in the 1930 *The Savoy Cocktail Book* called for a dash of orange bitters alongside gin and vermouth. Today, our orange bitters plays an essential role in brightening any modern Martini and adds an exuberant burst of elegant zestiness to this classic cocktail.

# MARTINI

Clean, zesty, delicious

The Martini is synonymous with old-school glamour and sophistication. Some may go so far as to say it's as American as apple pie. The closing scene of a movie is called the Martini shot, so is there a better way to celebrate a job well done?

**INGREDIENTS**
- 60ml gin
- 20ml dry vermouth
- 2 dashes of Angostura® orange bitters

**GARNISH**
* Lemon twist or pitted green olive

**GLASS**
* Martini, chilled

**METHOD**
1. Add all the ingredients to a mixing glass.
2. Half-fill with ice and stir for around 15 seconds until well chilled.
3. Strain into a chilled martini glass.
4. Garnish with a twist of lemon or a green olive, as you prefer.

*The secret to an excellent Martini is the temperature – the colder, the better. Keep your glass on ice before using it or put it in the freezer if you can. The best bars keep half of your Martini on ice while you're sipping on the first half. Some bars, such as Del Diego in Madrid, will continually change your glass for a fresh ice-cold one while you're talking to prevent your Martini ever becoming warm. It's the little details that make this drink.*

# MARTINEZ

Rich, herbal and spirited

A sophisticated cocktail that is a blend of a Manhattan and a Martini but actually predates the Martini. Today, maraschino steps in to provide the sweetness and body when using a modern London dry gin and the bitters provides depth and delicate spice. It was first published in 1884 in *The Modern Bartenders Guide* and is still well loved today.

### INGREDIENTS
- 45ml gin
- 45ml sweet vermouth
- 7ml maraschino liqueur
- 2 dashes of Angostura® aromatic bitters

### GARNISH
* Orange twist

### GLASS
* Coupe, chilled

### METHOD
1. Combine all the ingredients in a mixing glass.
2. Add some ice and stir until well chilled, around 15 seconds.
3. Strain into a chilled coupe glass.
4. Garnish with an orange twist.

> *Keep your cocktail glasses in the freezer or add a little ice to chill the glass while you're preparing the drink and then discard.*

# ROSITA

Bittersweet, zesty, spice

Bitter and boozy, this tequila twist on a Negroni was first published in 1974 but had a renaissance after being rediscovered by bar legend Gary 'Gaz' Regan. Quite possibly a 'perfect Negroni', this modern classic is much more complex than other takes, due to the split base of equal parts sweet and dry vermouth and the combination of bitters.

## INGREDIENTS
- 45ml reposado tequila
- 15ml Campari
- 15ml dry vermouth
- 15ml sweet vermouth
- 1 dash of Angostura® aromatic bitters
- 1 dash of Angostura® orange bitters

## GARNISH
* Twist of orange peel

## GLASS
* Rocks

## METHOD
1. Combine all the ingredients in a mixing glass.
2. Add some ice and stir well for around 20 seconds.
3. Strain into a rocks glass with a large ice cube.
4. Garnish with a twist of orange peel.

*Gaz Regan's legendary technique for stirring Negronis with his finger has been immortalised with a life-sized stainless-steel cast of his finger as a Negroni stirrer. Buy one or simply use your own finger!*

# FITZGERALD

Fresh, tangy, fragrant

Named after the American novelist F Scott Fitzgerald, this twist
on a gin sour with bitters and no egg white was first created by the
bartender Dale DeGroff, who spearheaded the craft cocktail scene
at the Rainbow Room in 1990s New York. This drink would have
been right at home at the legendary parties in The Great Gatsby.

### INGREDIENTS
- 50ml gin
- 20ml simple syrup
- 15ml fresh lemon juice
- 2 dashes of Angostura® aromatic bitters

### GARNISH
* Lemon twist

### GLASS
* Rocks

### METHOD
1. Add all the ingredients to a mixing glass.
2. Half-fill with ice and stir for around 15 seconds.
3. Strain into a rocks glass with ice.
4. Garnish with a lemon twist.

> *This is a gin sour without the egg, so if you love that
> fresh egg white fluffiness and texture, experiment with
> beating it in with a dry shake of the gin, lemon juice,
> bitters and simple syrup. Then add ice and
> shake again before straining into a coupe glass.*

# CHET BAKER

Velvety, honeyed, fruit

A liquid tribute to the legendary jazz musician Chet Baker, this is a sweeter take on an Old Fashioned, first created at Milk & Honey in New York. The use of rum in place of a spicier rye whiskey and the addition of honey syrup adds a soft sweetness – perfect to soothe those vocal cords. Like Chet Baker's tunes, there's no unnecessary flourishes here. Simplicity is the secret to this drink's success, which makes it so easy to try at home.

### INGREDIENTS
- 60ml aged rum
- 5ml honey syrup (see below)
- 10ml sweet vermouth
- 2 dashes of Angostura® aromatic bitters

### GARNISH
* Twist of orange peel

### GLASS
* Rocks

### METHOD
1. Combine all the ingredients in a mixing glass.
2. Add ice and stir well for around 20 seconds.
3. Strain over a large ice cube into a rocks glass.
4. Garnish with a twist of orange peel.

---

*To make honey syrup like a pro, dissolve three parts of the tastiest honey you can find with one part water over a low heat on the stove. Once dissolved, leave to cool.*

# MANDARIN SAZERAC

Citrus, vanilla, liquorice, spice

The classic Sazerac is named after a bar in New Orleans. This twist on a Sazerac uses mandarin liqueur to add a citrus lift and complement the vanilla and woody notes in the bourbon whiskey. These flavours are then bound together by a good few dashes of bitters. The classic Sazerac dates back to 1838 and, over a century later, it was crowned the official cocktail of New Orleans.

*Marco Nunes, Australia, Winner of Angostura® Global Cocktail Competition, 2006*

### INGREDIENTS
- 25ml La Fee NV Verte absinthe
- Chilled water
- 45ml Maker's Mark whiskey
- 15ml Mandarine Napoléon liqueur
- 3 dashes of Angostura® aromatic bitters
- 5ml simple syrup

### GARNISH
* Lemon and mandarin peel

### GLASS
* Nick & Nora

### METHOD
1. Rinse a chilled cocktail glass with the absinthe and chilled water (see below).
2. Add the remaining ingredients to a cocktail shaker with ice.
3. Shake well for around 15 seconds.
4. Strain into the absinthe-rinsed Nick & Nora glass.
5. Garnish with lemon and mandarin peel.

---

*To rinse a cocktail glass with absinthe and water, combine the two liquids and swirl around a chilled cocktail glass. Then discard the liquid.*

# OAXACA OLD FASHIONED

Smoke, pepper, spice

This is a riff on an Old Fashioned using a split base of tequila and mezcal, which is actually quite old fashioned in its approach. Old Fashioneds used to be made with all manner of spirits; it's only in the modern era where whiskey has laid claim to be the default base. It's one of the first modern classic cocktails that calls for mezcal. Within just a couple of years of its creation at New York's Death & Co, an Old Fashioned that was made with tequila and mezcal was adopted by bars internationally.

### INGREDIENTS
- 45ml reposado tequila
- 15ml mezcal
- 2 dashes of Angostura® aromatic bitters
- 5ml agave nectar

### GARNISH
* Flamed orange peel twist (see below)

### GLASS
* Rocks

### METHOD
1. Add all the ingredients to a rocks glass with one large ice cube.
2. Stir for around 15 seconds until well chilled.
3. Garnish with a flamed orange peel twist.

---

*To make a flamed orange peel twist, cut a 5cm round of orange peel and hold it, skin-side down, above the drink. Light a match and use it to warm the skin-side of the peel. Squeeze the twist towards the match and the spritz of oil from the twist will briefly burst into flames. Then, drop the flamed twist into the drink.*

# THE SCARLET IBIS

Cherry, herbal, smoke

The Scarlet Ibis is named after Trinidad and Tobago's national bird in a tribute to the wonderful scarlet colour the five dashes of bitters brings to the drink. The smoky whisky combines with the burnt sugar notes of the Madeira and the honeyed sweetness of yellow chartreuse, while the ripe black cherries and bitters bring extra depth of flavour.

*Andrew Griffiths, Australia, Winner Angostura® Global Cocktail Competition, 2011*

### INGREDIENTS

- 2 fresh black cherries, pitted
- A pinch of sea salt
- 60ml Bunnahabhain 12 year old whisky
- 15ml aged Madeira
- 10ml yellow chartreuse
- 5 dashes of Angostura® aromatic bitters

### GARNISH

* Drunk cherry oysters

### GLASS

* Martini, chilled

### METHOD

1. Muddle the cherries and salt in a large glass jug.
2. Add the remaining ingredients and let it sit to infuse.
3. Stir with large chunks of ice.
4. Strain into a chilled martini glass.
5. Garnish with drunk cherry oysters (see below).

---

*To make drunk cherry oysters, take the shredded cherries from the bottom of the jug and combine them with a dash of whisky and a pinch of salt.*

---

# OLD FLAME

Spice, sweet, rich fruit

Old Flame perfectly captures the sweet vibrancy and exuberance of Trinidad and Tobago. At its base is Angostura® 1824 rum, which boasts lovely dark fruit, vanilla and spice notes, with heat from the chilli-infused sherry and an aromatic lift from the orange bitters. It is a deceptively simple drink with layers upon layers of flavour that can be made by anyone anywhere.

*Ray Letoa, New Zealand, Angostura® Global Cocktail Competition winner, 2018*

### INGREDIENTS
- 45ml Angostura® 1824 rum
- 15ml chilli-infused Pedro Ximénez sherry (see below)
- 5 dashes of Angostura® aromatic bitters
- 2 dashes of Angostura® orange bitters

### GARNISH
* Orange zest and a chilli ganache chocolate

### GLASS
* Rocks

### METHOD
1. Add all the ingredients to a rocks glass.
2. Add a large ice cube and stir for 10 seconds or until well chilled.
3. Garnish with the orange zest and a chilli ganache chocolate.

> *To infuse Pedro Ximénez sherry with chilli, cut 2 fresh red chillies and leave to infuse in 400ml of sherry for 24 hours at room temperature. Strain and bottle.*

# TWIN CITIES

Rich, fruity and soft spice

The Twin Cities was created for Dead Rabbit's 2022 taproom menu and uses a fig leaf-infused blend of Irish and American whiskey, Keeper's Heart, which is round, fruity and spicy. The fig infusion works well with the coconut and vanilla notes from the ex-bourbon barrels the whiskey was aged in and apricot brightens the nutty tones. Essentially a riff on a Manhattan with an Irish twist, this subs rye for the softer Irish American whiskey.

### INGREDIENTS
- 40ml fig leaf-infused Keeper's Heart Irish + American Whiskey
- (see below)
- 15ml Pierre Ferrand 1840 cognac
- 7ml Giffard Abricot du Roussillon (apricot liqueur)
- 30ml Cocchi Vermouth di Torino
- ½ tsp verjus blanc
- 2 dashes of Angostura® cocoa bitters

### GLASS
* Nick & Nora

### METHOD
1. Add all the ingredients to a mixing glass.
2. Half-fill with ice and stir for around 15 seconds until well chilled.
3. Strain into a Nick & Nora glass.

---

*To make fig leaf-infused Keeper's Heart Irish + American Whiskey, combine 750ml of the whiskey, 15g fresh fig leaves and 15g dried fig leaves in a container with a tight-fitting lid. Steep for 2 hours at room temperature before straining and storing in a sterilised glass bottle.*

---

# I'M NOT DRINKING, BUT
# MAKE IT DELICIOUS

Not drinking does not mean you have to miss out. This chapter will help you prepare alcohol-free drinks as delicious as their full-strength counterparts. All the recipes here have been compiled with the same creativity, care and attention as the rest of the book and contain less than 0.05 per cent abv, as our bitters has only trace amounts of alcohol.

You'll find alcohol-free twists on classic cocktails, drinks you'll recognise, as well as new innovative concoctions. If you're a fan of a Negroni, try our No-groni. If a creamy Piña Colada is more your speed, check out the Nut Ah Colada. If you're looking to celebrate, try the Winter 75, an alcohol-free twist on a French parfait!

## A STORY IN EVERY DASH:
## THE LEMON, LIME AND BITTERS

Australia lays claim to first discovering the refreshing delight that comes with combining lemon, lime and bitters.

Bitters-based refreshers were already popular in Victorian England when Carlos Siegert, son of the founder of Angostura, visited Australia in 1879 as part of a promotional tour. But it was Australia that added the lime to the mix.

Angostura® lemon, lime and bitters is the original adult non-alcoholic drink and a reported 100 million are served in Australian bars each year. It's traditional to enjoy the drink after a round of golf, although these days it is more likely to be enjoyed while watching a game of cricket or chilling on the beach or at a barbecue.

Australia's overwhelming adoption of bitters mixed with lemon, lime and soda inspired Angostura to bottle this refreshing combination in 2007 and later create the Chill line of vibrant, modern bitters-based refreshers.

# LEMON, LIME AND BITTERS

Citrus, tangy, refreshing

The perfect marriage of the tart sweetness of a lemon-lime soda with the intricate flavour profile of bitters. Lemon, Lime and Bitters is affectionately known by some as LLB, or 'Lime Like a Boss' in Trinidad. Lime is not just some fruit in Trinidad, it's a term that means to party or chill with friends.

### INGREDIENTS
- 1 tbsp fresh lime juice
- 250ml lemonade
- 3–4 dashes of Angostura® aromatic bitters

### GARNISH
* Lime wedges

### GLASS
* Highball

### METHOD
1. Fill a highball glass full of ice.
2. Squeeze in the fresh lime juice and top with the lemonade.
3. Add the bitters.
4. Stir gently and garnish with a lime wedge.

---

*The Angostura® Chill line up of bitters-based refreshers comes in a few different flavours, including Blood Orange & Bitters and Caribbean Sorrel (aka hibiscus) & Bitters. Experiment with your favourite refreshing flavour and add lemonade, lime and bitters to create your own variation.*

# WINTER 75

Citrus, spice, effervescent

An elegant sparkling blend of citrus and warming winter spice topped with alcohol-free sparkling wine that's ideal for holiday celebrations. This zero-proof twist on a classic French 75 by the queen of low and no alcohol cocktails, Camille Vidal, hits with remarkable precision. The French 75 is a classic celebratory drink, traditionally served on New Year's Eve in France, where it is simply called the *Soixante-quinze*.

*Camille Vidal aka @mindfullycami at @lamaisonwellness*

### INGREDIENTS
- 15ml allspice syrup
- 15ml fresh lemon juice
- 2 dashes of Angostura® orange bitters
- Alcohol-free sparkling wine, to top

### GARNISH
* Pared orange zest

### GLASS
* Champagne flute

### METHOD
1. Combine the allspice syrup and lemon juice in a Champagne flute and stir.
2. Add the bitters.
3. Top with alcohol-free sparkling wine and garnish with pared orange zest.

*Serve the sparkling wine ice-cold to retain those beautiful bubbles for longer.*

# FRUITY BUCK

Bright, tangy, vibrant

The founder of Milk & Honey, Sasha Petraske, always said that in order to make a great mocktail, simply double the measurements of the non-alcoholic ingredients of a drink. By doing this, you'll have made a fantastic and versatile base that you can tweak and twist to make a non-alcoholic drink that truly suits your taste. What spin would you put on this fresh, tangy and fruity serve?

### INGREDIENTS
- 30ml fresh pineapple juice
- 15ml fresh lime juice
- 15ml fresh lemon juice
- 1 tsp agave syrup
- 2 dashes of Angostura® aromatic bitters
- 90ml soda water

### GLASS
* Collins

### METHOD
1. Combine all the ingredients, except the soda, in a cocktail shaker.
2. Add some ice and shake well for around 15 seconds.
3. Add the soda water and pour into a Collins glass filled with ice.

# GREEN MIND COLLINS

Fresh, herbal, citrus

A great Dry January drink, this is a refreshing, biting blend of celery syrup and lemon and apple juices with a couple of dashes of bitters to add depth and bind the flavours together, then topped with soda. A twist on a Tom Collins without the gin, it's thirst-quenching, full of flavour and ideal for when you need a clear head.

*Camille Vidal aka @mindfullycami at @lamaisonwellness*

### INGREDIENTS
- 25ml fresh lemon juice
- 50ml fresh apple juice
- 5ml celery syrup
- 2 dashes of Angostura® aromatic bitters
- Soda water, to top

### GARNISH
* Apple fan (see below)

### GLASS
* Collins

### METHOD
1. Fill a Collins glass with ice.
2. Add the lemon and apple juices, celery syrup and bitters.
3. Stir gently.
4. Top with soda water and garnish with an apple fan.

*To make an apple fan, slice an apple in half from top to bottom and remove the core. Lay one half, cut side down, on a chopping board and cut into thin slices. Remove the first slice, then take 3 or 5 apple slices (odd numbers look better) and fan them out from the top. Use a cocktail stick to skewer the fan and hold it in place.*

# SOBER SUMMER CUP

Fruity, refreshing, fragrant

This is an alcohol-free twist on a Pimm's No 1 cup, a refreshing sharing serve that signals the start of summer in the UK and is synonymous with Wimbledon. A healthy measure of fresh lemon juice coupled with dashes of bitters provide the tartness and spicy depth of flavour without the need for alcohol. The Victorians used to blend fruit and spices in a homemade punch-style summer serve, garnished with fresh fruit to make a summery fruit cup.

### INGREDIENTS

- 4 fresh mint leaves
- 100ml lemon- lime soda
- 6 cucumber slices
- 2 fresh strawberries, quartered
- 2 lemon wedges
- 50ml ginger ale
- 25ml cola
- 25ml fresh orange juice
- 1 tbsp fresh lemon juice
- 2 dashes of Angostura® aromatic bitters

### GARNISH

* Cucumber slices, halved fresh strawberries, fresh mint leaves and a lemon wheel

### GLASS

* Highball

### METHOD

1. Muddle the mint leaves in a highball glass.
2. Add half of the lemon-lime soda and the rest of the ingredients.
3. Stir to combine.
4. Chill in the fridge for 3 hours to allow the flavours to combine.
5. To serve, add some ice and the remaining lemon-lime soda.
6. Garnish with cucumber slices, strawberry halves, mint leaves and a lemon wheel.

> *The Sober Summer Cup is designed to be shared, so simply multiply the ingredients by the number of guests and serve in a glass jug with a big wooden spoon to allow for a quick stir before pouring out each glass.*

# 4-WAY CITRUS SHRUB

Citrus, fresh, vibrant

This is a twist on a Lemon, Lime and Bitters (see page 126) that is all about using leftover citrus peels and husks. We've used lemons, limes, grapefruits and oranges but you can use any citrus fruit you'd like. This drink taps into the trends for zero waste and alcohol-free cocktails, so it's a real feel-good drink.

*Rohan Massie, Tasmania, 2021*

### INGREDIENTS
- 30ml 4-way citrus shrub (see below)
- 3–4 dashes of Angostura® aromatic bitters
- Soda water, to top

### GARNISH
* Citrus fruit wedge

### GLASS
* Collins

### METHOD
1. Build all the ingredients in a Collins glass over ice.
2. Top with soda water and garnish with a citrus fruit wedge.

---

*To make the 4-way citrus shrub, take about 1 handful of waste citrus peels and husks. Combine with 500g caster sugar, give it all a light massage to get the oils flowing and leave, covered, overnight. The next day, add 750ml hot water (approximately the temperature you would drink tea at) and stir to dissolve the sugar. Strain out the fruit and add 50ml Chardonnay vinegar to provide acidity. Pour the shrub into a sterilised glass bottle and seal. Cool, then keep in the fridge for up to 2 weeks.*

---

# NUT AH COLADA

Tropical, rich, creamy

The Piña Colada sings of summer days – one sip and your mind immediately escapes to a beach. No need to miss out if you're not drinking, this alcohol-free version includes a little peanut butter along with coconut cream and the earthy richness of cocoa bitters to provide the depth of flavour.

**INGREDIENTS**
- 4 dashes of Angostura® cocoa bitters
- 90ml fresh pineapple juice
- 1 tsp smooth peanut butter
- 30ml coconut cream
- 30ml full-fat milk

**GARNISH**
* An edible flower and citrus twist

**GLASS**
* Highball

**METHOD**
1. Add the bitters and all the remaining ingredients to a cocktail shaker.
2. Add some ice and shake well for around 20 seconds.
3. Double strain into a highball glass filled with ice.
4. Garnish with an edible flower and a citrus twist.

*Use creamy peanut butter instead of crunchy for a smooth, rich, sweet depth to this drink.*

# AMARETTI SOUR

Almond, sweet, sour, velvety

An Amaretto Sour without the alcohol, thanks to the smart folk at Lyre's who have figured out how to create sober versions of many of our favourite full-strength spirits. This is a delicious, short, grown-up drink that offers a fancy experience for those not drinking. The Amaretto Sour came of age in the 1970s and is one of the few brand-created classics.

### INGREDIENTS
- 75ml Lyre's amaretti
- 15ml fresh lemon juice
- 5ml simple syrup
- 10ml egg white
- 3 dashes of Angostura® aromatic bitters

### GARNISH
* Lemon wedge and maraschino cherry

### GLASS
* Rocks

### METHOD
1. Add all the ingredients to a shaker.
2. Fill with ice and shake hard and fast for 20 seconds.
3. Strain into a rocks glass.
4. Add fresh ice and garnish with a lemon wedge and maraschino cherry.

---

*Vegan? Use aquafaba in place of egg white. To make aquafaba, drain a can of cooked chickpeas and, using a hand-held electric mixer, whip up the liquid for 3–6 minutes until it forms soft peaks. There you have it, a vegan, egg-free alternative to egg white that provides the same lovely texture in sours.*

# NO-GRONI

Bittersweet, herbal, citrus

A classic aperitif from the Latin, *aperire*, a Negroni is designed to open up your stomach ahead of dinner. But you don't need alcohol to help stimulate your appetite. The No-groni will do the same job and tastes just as delicious. This is probably one of the few new classic alcohol-free cocktails.

### INGREDIENTS
- 30ml Seedlip Spice 94 or an alcohol-free gin
- 30ml Giffard apéritif syrup
- 30ml Lyre's apéritif rosso
- 2 dashes of Angostura® orange bitters
- 2 dashes of Angostura® aromatic bitters

### GARNISH
* Orange twist

### GLASS
* Rocks

### METHOD
1. Add all the ingredients to a mixing glass.
2. Half-fill with ice and stir until well chilled, around 15 seconds.
3. Strain into a rocks glass filled with ice.
4. Garnish with an orange twist.

> *This is a great drink to batch in advance and simply pour when ready to serve for minimal fuss and maximum flavour when hosting.*

# OBELIX

Fruity, fresh, effervescent

This is a bold, mesmerising blend of tangy fruit, bitters and soda. The intense bold botanicals of the bitters shine through alongside fresh pineapple and lime juice, raspberry syrup and a good splash of Schweppes Russchian pink soda.

*Antonia Lo Casto, Italy, Angostura Global Cocktail Challenge winner, 2011*

### INGREDIENTS
- 20ml fresh pineapple juice
- 5ml lime syrup
- 5ml raspberry syrup
- 20ml Schweppes Russchian pink soda
- 3 dashes of Angostura® aromatic bitters

### GARNISH
* Slices of apple and lime, a twist of orange peel and pineapple leaves

### GLASS
* Tumbler

### METHOD
1. Combine all the ingredients in the tumbler.
2. Add ice.
3. Stir gently.
4. Garnish with slices of apple and lime, a twist of orange peel and pineapple leaves.

---

*If you're struggling to find Schweppes Russchian pink soda, which includes a tantalising mix of red berries, hibiscus and carrot, try a good-quality pink lemonade and half the measure of raspberry syrup.*

---

# APERITIFS

Aperitifs are drinks designed to open the appetite, so are ideal to enjoy before or with food. They often include ingredients with a lighter abv, such as vermouths, sherries, bitter liqueurs, or the bourbon highball. They are also very well diluted with a 4:1 or 5:1 ratio of whiskey to soda to allow a light, refreshing start to proceedings before the stomach is suitably lined.

Italian aperitivo culture has exploded globally in recent years and the Negroni has gone from a bartender secret to global phenomenon. Here we've got a great twist on the Negroni in the form of a Cacao Negroni using a rose-scented gin.

Different countries have different drinks that are traditional as aperitifs. In Spain, for example, vermouth is a popular aperitif ingredient. Frequently enjoyed simply on the rocks or in a special local concoction often involving a splash of gin and soda, the Media Combinación pays homage to this rustic style of Spanish aperitif.

# A STORY IN EVERY DASH:
# THE PINK GIN

One of the earliest cocktails to be made with bitters was the Pink Gin. It was created by sailors who started drinking bitters to combat stomach ailments. However, they soon discovered that adding a dash or two of bitters to their daily officer ration of Plymouth gin made a delicious drink.

The Pink Gin cocktail is traditionally served warm or at room temperature and undiluted as a testament to its nautical origins, as there would not be ice readily available on board ships in the nineteenth century.

# PINK GIN

Aromatic, citrus, herbal

The Pink Gin was originally created out of necessity by Royal Navy officers who were looking for something to sweeten on-board bitters prescribed to settle their stomachs and quell seasickness. The marriage of botanical gin and aromatic bitters took place in the mid-1820s, way before the gin and tonic became a thing.

**INGREDIENTS**
- 60ml gin
- 3 dashes of Angostura® aromatic bitters

**GARNISH**
* Lemon peel

**GLASS**
* Coupe, chilled

**METHOD**
1. In a mixing glass, stir both ingredients with ice to chill.
2. Strain into a chilled coupe glass.
3. Express the oils from the lemon peel over the cocktail and use the peel to garnish.

> *While traditionally served warm or at room temperature, there are two ways to serve up a Pink Gin. You can prepare it as described above, or you might prefer to swirl a few dashes of bitters to coat a chilled glass before adding the gin.*

# VIEJÍSIMO ADONIS

Opulent, rich, dried fruit

This Viejísimo Adonis, or 'very old Adonis', is a spectacle at 1862 Dry Bar – a bar named after the year that Jerry Thomas's first bartender guide was published. The Adonis is the original low-alcohol cocktail that is often 'thrown', a traditional Spanish technique used to aerate and amplify aromatics in wine-based ingredients such as sherry and vermouth. It was created around 1885 by Joseph F McKone to celebrate a popular Broadway show called Adonis.

*Alberto Martinez, 1862Dry Bar, Madrid, 2017*

### INGREDIENTS
- 45ml Lustau amontillado VORS
- 45ml Lustau red vermouth
- 1 tsp Lustau Cream East India Solera sherry
- 2 dashes of Angostura® orange bitters

### GARNISH
* Pitted green olive and an orange twist

### GLASS
* Nick & Nora

### METHOD
1. Assemble your cocktail in one tin of your two-parts cocktail shaker. Include ice and hold a strainer to avoid it from falling out.
2. Hold that tin (the 'throwing' one) with one hand over your head.
3. This hand will stay still. Hold the other tin (the 'receiving' one) with the other hand as far down as possible. Now you are ready.
4. Keeping your throwing hand up, bring the receiving tin up to start pouring. During this pouring, slowly lower the receiving tin as far down as you can until all the liquid has been transferred.
5. Repeat this process four or five times, then pour into a Nick & Nora glass.
6. Garnish with a green olive and an orange twist.

> *This is a great cocktail to batch in advance and then throw around to liven up before serving.*

# BAMBOO

Bone-dry, savoury, citrus

The Bamboo was created by bartender Louis Eppinger in San Francisco as early as 1886. The 50:50 ratio of dry vermouth to fino sherry makes it a beautifully balanced, elegant, complex cocktail. The Bamboo is the second great sherry-vermouth drink that was inspired by the success of the Manhattan and bartenders' desire to create a lower-proof drink.

### INGREDIENTS
- 45ml fino sherry
- 45ml dry vermouth
- 1 dash of Angostura® aromatic bitters
- 1 dash of Angostura® orange bitters

### GARNISH
* Lemon twist

### GLASS
* Coupe, chilled

### METHOD
1. Add all the ingredients to a mixing glass.
2. Half-fill with ice and stir for 15 seconds or until well chilled.
3. Strain into a chilled coupe glass and garnish with a lemon twist.

*Sherry is delicious and incredibly good value. It's wonderful in cocktails and with food. The salinity of a fino gives the wine a savoury umami note, which means it can stand up to big complex foods where some wines would struggle. It works really well with sushi or mushroom dishes and its tanginess can stand up to olives and cured meats. Once opened, fino is best refrigerated and consumed within a few days.*

# BOOTHBY COCKTAIL

*Decadent, richly aromatic*

An eponymous cocktail, The Boothby was created by San Francisco bartender William T Boothby, who was also known as 'Cocktail Bill'. The Boothby is essentially a Manhattan Royale – rye, sweet vermouth and bitters lengthened with Champagne. It's been around since at least 1891 and is still being enjoyed today.

### INGREDIENTS
- 60ml rye whiskey or bourbon
- 30ml sweet vermouth
- 2 dashes of Angostura® orange bitters
- 1 dash of Angostura® aromatic bitters
- 30ml Champagne

### GARNISH
* Maraschino cherry

### GLASS
* Coupe, chilled

### METHOD
1. Combine the whiskey, vermouth and bitters in a mixing glass.
2. Half-fill with ice and stir until well chilled for around 15 seconds.
3. Strain into a chilled coupe glass.
4. Top with the Champagne and garnish with a maraschino cherry.

> *Using rye gives more of a crisp, spicy bite,*
> *while bourbon leads to a softer drink.*

# TRINITY

Bittersweet and aromatic

The Trinity is so-called for the trio of French dry vermouth, Italian sweet vermouth and three dashes of bitters. It was featured in the 1924 Angostura® Bitters *Centenary Cocktail Book*, published to celebrate our 100th anniversary. It's perhaps not a classic now, but maybe it's time for a revival …

### INGREDIENTS
- 30ml gin
- 30ml French dry vermouth
- 30ml Italian sweet vermouth
- 3 dashes of Angostura® aromatic bitters

### GARNISH
* Lemon twist

### GLASS
* Rocks

### METHOD
1. Combine all the ingredients in a rocks glass.
2. Add ice and stir gently.
3. Garnish with a twist of lemon.

> *Keep your vermouth in the fridge. Vermouth is a fortified wine, which means that once you open the bottle, the exposure to air or more oxygen causes a reaction that changes the flavour profile … and not for the better. The best way to slow this process is to refrigerate your vermouth once opened. This will help it stay vibrant and fresher for longer.*

# MEDIA COMBINACIÓN

Bittersweet, fragrant, citrus

This rustic Spanish drink mixes vermouth and gin (or any other spirit) and topped with any number of garnishes. It was born in the post-war era when resources were scarce and people wanted an aperitif cocktail that made use of the plentiful resources at the time: gin and vermouth.

### INGREDIENTS
- 60ml Spanish red vermouth
- 30ml London dry gin
- 7ml orange curaçao
- 2 dashes of Angostura® aromatic bitters

### GARNISH
* Orange peel and a pitted green olive

### GLASS
* Rocks

### METHOD
1. Add all the ingredients to a rocks glass full of ice.
2. Stir gently.
3. Express the oils from the orange peel into the drink.
4. Twist the orange peel and place in the glass.
5. Garnish with the green olive.

# THE CHARMER

Herbal, sweet, tangy

This drink is how Daniyel Jones charmed himself into a job as Angostura® ambassador after wowing judges with his freestyle cocktail at our Global Cocktail Competition in 2013. The combination of rum, Bénédictine liqueur, sherry vinegar and lime juice is balanced by honey and five dashes of bitters. The foam finish makes this drink fancy. It is tantalising on the tongue but deceptively simple to make.

*Daniyel Jones, Trinidad and Tobago Angostura Global Cocktail Challenge winner, 2013, now Angostura® ambassador*

### INGREDIENTS
- 45ml Angostura® 5 year old rum
- 20ml Bénédictine liqueur
- 10ml sherry vinegar
- 10ml fresh lime juice
- 1 bar spoon of organic honey
- 5 dashes of Angostura® aromatic bitters

### GARNISH
* Bay leaf foam (see below)

### GLASS
* Nick & Nora, chilled

### METHOD
1. Add all the ingredients to a cocktail shaker.
2. Half-fill with ice and shake for 10–15 seconds until chilled.
3. Strain and serve into a chilled Nick & Nora glass.
4. Garnish with the bay leaf foam.

---

*To make a bay leaf foam, add 4 egg whites, 85g Angostura® aromatic bitters, 85g honey infused with bay leaves for 14 days, 25g lemon juice and 55g water to an iSi Whipper, then cap and shake to mix. Charge the iSi Whipper twice, shaking between charges. Chill for at least 1 hour before use.*

---

# BOURBON HIGHBALL

Light, zesty, refreshing

This refreshingly simple combination of bourbon, soda and a dash of orange bitters is the perfect aperitif for whiskey fans. Served ice cold, this is a great pre-dinner drink and also has enough acidity to accompany fatty fried foods. The highball is an aperitif that originated in the UK, was popularised in the US and perfected into an artform in Japan.

### INGREDIENTS
- 40ml bourbon
- 120ml soda water
- 1 dash of Angostura® orange bitters

### GARNISH
* Orange twist

### GLASS
* Highball

### METHOD
1. Add the bourbon to a highball glass filled with ice.
2. Top with the soda.
3. Add the bitters and gently stir.
4. Garnish with an orange twist.

*Chill the soda and pour over the back of a spoon along the side of the glass, avoiding direct contact with the ice to help retain the bubbles in the soda.*

# CUBAN CHAWARI

Fragrant, fresh, spice

Chawari means 'cut with tea' and is a variation on another aperitif, a Mizuwari, which means 'cut with water'. It's a traditional way to enjoy a whisky or shochu in Japan. In this iteration, rum is paired with tea and spiked with flavourful accents. It was created at Kwãnt Mayfair, which attracts the best in the cocktail industry from all over the world.

*Gento Torigata, Kwãnt Mayfair, London, 2023*

### INGREDIENTS
- 40ml Caribbean spiced rum
- 60ml Taiwanese black tea (see below)
- 5ml oloroso sherry
- 3ml agave nectar
- 1ml Muyu jasmine verte liqueur
- 2 dashes of Angostura® aromatic bitters

### GLASS
* Nick & Nora

### METHOD
1. Combine all the ingredients in a cocktail shaker.
2. Add some ice and stir to pre-chill the mix.
3. Pour into a Nick & Nora glass with a large ice cube.

> *Brew the tea with a ratio of 4g tea leaves to 100ml hot water (90°C) for 5 minutes, then strain and cool before use.*

# CACAO NEGRONI

Bittersweet, rose and dark chocolate

The Negroni has found new fame in recent years and this rose version uses a double measure of South African Bayab rose water gin, rose vermouth, cacao-infused Campari and a couple of dashes of cocoa bitters. The Negroni dates back to the 1920s when Count Camillo Negroni ordered his Americano to be made with gin rather than soda water.

### INGREDIENTS
- 60ml Bayab rose water gin
- 30ml rose vermouth
- 30ml cacao-infused Campari (see below)
- 2 dashes of Angostura® cocoa bitters

### GARNISH
* Orange twist

### GLASS
* Rocks

### METHOD
1. Combine all the ingredients in a rocks glass.
2. Add a large ice cube.
3. Stir until well chilled, around 15 seconds.
4. Garnish with a twist of orange.

*To make the cacao-infused Campari, simply add 1 tablespoon of fresh cacao pods to a bottle of Campari and leave overnight. Remove the cacao and strain.*

# DIGESTIFS

After-dinner cocktails were traditionally drinks that would
help you digest your meal and would often include any
number of bitter liqueurs, herbs and spices thought to help calm
the stomach. The classy Champs-Élysées includes cognac
and is a classic post-dinner drink with the herbal green chartreuse,
lemon, bitters and a touch of sugar.

The Bijou or Doctor's Orders could easily replace dessert and
provide the same sweet lift often appreciated at the end of a meal.

And, if you're a fan of a cheeseboard, there is the perfect Manhattan,
made with a British brandy and garnished with a slice of pecorino.

Coffee is a big post-dinner occasion and here we have three
coffee-based cocktails: a rich bitter chocolate take on an Espresso
Martini, a Mr Brown, an invigorating blend of bourbon and
coffee, and a Café Trinidad, the island's answer to an Irish coffee.

# A STORY IN EVERY DASH: THE ESPRESSO MARTINI

The Espresso Martini is a modern classic cocktail created by the godfather of the London cocktail scene, Dick Bradsell. The creation of the drink is part of modern cocktail folklore. Around 1983, a budding supermodel requested a drink that would simultaneously wake her up and, ahem, mess her up.

The Espresso Martini has experienced a revival in recent years – it was one of the most ordered cocktails in US bars in 2023. Using fresh espresso and a long hard shake is the best way to create the signature froth, which takes a good amount of work on a busy evening.

Nowadays, there are even more choices in terms of quality coffee liqueurs and cocoa bitters to accent this modern classic. The signature three coffee beans atop an Espresso Martini signify health, wealth and happiness.

# ESPRESSO MARTINI

Rich, bitter, sweet

This was originally known as a Vodka Espresso and later as the pharmaceutical stimulant before finally being crowned the Espresso Martini. It seemingly fails to go out of fashion, as coffee and spirit is a winning combination. A true modern classic, a drink that is replicated around the world and is a true bar call. Whether it's on menus or not, people will ask for it!

### INGREDIENTS
- 45ml vodka
- 15ml coffee liqueur
- 30ml freshly brewed espresso coffee
- 15ml simple syrup
- 6 dashes of Angostura® cocoa bitters

### GARNISH
* 3 coffee beans

### GLASS
* Coupe, chilled

### METHOD
1. Pour all the ingredients into a cocktail shaker.
2. Add ice and shake vigorously for 20 seconds until nice and frothy.
3. Strain into a chilled coupe glass and garnish with the coffee beans.

---

*The trick to a good Espresso Martini is in the frothy head. For this, you need to use a good-quality espresso that will have the right oils and shake it vigorously, then let the foam settle in your glass before you garnish.*

# BIJOU

Bright, sweet and herbaceous

A real jewel of a drink, Bijou includes a trio of ingredients that shine like gems with an accent of orange bitters. Bijou translates as jewel and is inspired by the hues of the drink's three main components: gin for diamond, sweet vermouth for ruby and green chartreuse for emerald. One of the earliest cocktails to call for orange bitters, the Bijou cocktail is a Harry Johnson creation from 1900.

**INGREDIENTS**
- 45ml gin
- 20ml sweet vermouth
- 20ml green chartreuse
- 2 dashes of Angostura® orange bitters

**GARNISH**
* Lemon twist

**GLASS**
* Coupe, chilled

**METHOD**
1. Combine all the ingredients in a mixing glass.
2. Add ice and stir until well chilled, around 15 seconds.
3. Strain into a chilled coupe glass.
4. Garnish with a lemon twist.

# CHAMPS-ÉLYSÉES

Light, citrusy, herbaceous

Named after the famous Parisian avenue, this is an elegant variation on a Sidecar where a herbal green chartreuse is used in place of zesty curaçao. This substitution is, as the French would say, a triomphe! First published in 1925, the team at Milk & Honey in New York had a hand in reviving this classic.

### INGREDIENTS
- 45ml cognac
- 15ml green chartreuse
- 20ml fresh lemon juice
- 15ml simple syrup
- 3–4 dashes of Angostura® aromatic bitters

### GARNISH
* Strip of pared lemon peel

### GLASS
* Coupe or Nick & Nora, chilled

### METHOD
1. Combine all the ingredients in a cocktail shaker with ice.
2. Shake well.
3. Strain into a chilled coupe or Nick & Nora glass.
4. Garnish with a strip of lemon peel.

> *Use a young VS cognac for more of those fragrant, floral fruity notes and not an XO cognac which will have too complex a flavour profile that could overpower this drink.*

# BLACK MANHATTAN

Bittersweet, aromatic, strong

This is an inspired simple switch. In a Black Manhattan, sweet vermouth is subbed for the richer, bittersweet herbal amaro, which bartenders in the US were getting a taste for back in 2005. This is a really easy, intensely-flavoured drink for a professional or home bartender.

**INGREDIENTS**
- 60ml rye whiskey
- 30ml amaro
- 1 dash of Angostura® aromatic bitters
- 1 dash of Angostura® orange bitters

**GARNISH**
* Maraschino cherry

**GLASS**
* Coupe, chilled

**METHOD**
1. Combine all the ingredients in a mixing glass.
2. Add some ice and stir well.
3. Strain into chilled coupe glass.
4. Garnish with a maraschino cherry.

> *This drink was originally made with Averna amaro, but there are so many different styles of amaro, so play around with what you have at home and see what difference it makes.*

# MR BROWN

Silky, strong, indulgent

Mr Brown is the perfect nightcap – a blend of bourbon and coffee liqueur with a touch of vanilla syrup and a dash of aromatic and orange bitters. The name is inspired by the Quentin Tarantino film Reservoir Dogs, as there's a particular scene that anyone working in hospitality will remember well. First created by Frankie Marshall at the Clover Club in New York, this will no doubt become a modern classic due to its simplicity but complex layers of flavour.

### INGREDIENTS
- 60ml bourbon
- 20ml coffee liqueur, preferably coffee herring
- 5ml vanilla syrup (see below)
- 1 dash of Angostura® aromatic bitters
- 1 dash of Angostura® orange bitters

### GARNISH
* Orange twist

### GLASS
* Rocks

### METHOD
1. Combine all the ingredients in a mixing glass.
2. Add some ice and stir for around 45 seconds until well chilled.
3. Strain into a rocks glass over a large ice cube.
4. Garnish with an orange twist.

---

*To make your own vanilla syrup, combine 1 split vanilla pod with equal measures of water and sugar in a saucepan over a medium heat, then stir until sugar has dissolved. Remove from the heat and let it cool. Remove the vanilla pod and store in a sterilised glass bottle, where it will keep for around 2 weeks.*

# CAFÉ TRINIDAD

Sweet, rich, coffee

This is a Trinidad twist on an Irish coffee, where instead of whiskey there are several dashes of orange and cocoa bitters added to a sweet, chilled coffee with that signature cool, cream float. The result is a less boozy but equally flavoursome drink that is perfect after a meal. Trinidadians love adding bitters to their morning brew, so this is a very Trini take on an after-dinner drink.

### INGREDIENTS
- 60ml chilled espresso
- 22.5ml demerara syrup (see page 96)
- 2 dashes of Angostura® orange bitters
- 6 dashes of Angostura® cocoa bitters
- Double cream, slightly whipped

### GARNISH
* Grated nutmeg and an edible flower

### GLASS
* Champagne flute, chilled

### METHOD
1. Add all the ingredients to a cocktail shaker, except the double cream.
2. Shake with some ice.
3. Strain into a chilled Champagne flute.
4. Float the cream on top (see below).
5. Garnish with a dusting of grated nutmeg and an edible flower.

*Whip the double cream just a little so it has a thick texture, but not too much, then pour over the back of a spoon to help it float.*

# DOCTOR'S ORDERS

Fresh, fruity, pungent

This could easily be a delicious liquid dessert – beautifully balanced, sweet and fruity with freshness and texture. This drink celebrates simplicity and technique – creatively pairing simple flavours and classic techniques can produce a perfect drink without the need for any fancy bar equipment.

*Rohan Massie, Tasmania Angostura® Global Cocktail Competition finalist, 2020*

### INGREDIENTS

- 50ml Angostura® 5 year old rum
- 10 fresh basil leaves
- 20ml strawberry cordial (see below)
- 40ml fresh mandarin juice
- 30ml coconut milk
- 5ml fresh lime juice
- 2 dashes of Angostura® orange bitters

### GARNISH

* Sprigs of fresh basil and freeze-dried mandarin segments

### GLASS

* Diver

### METHOD

1. Add all the ingredients to a cocktail shaker.
2. Top with some ice cubes.
3. Short shake for 5 seconds.
4. Double strain over crushed ice in a pearl diver glass.
5. Garnish with basil sprigs and freeze-dried mandarin segments.

---

*To make a strawberry cordial, combine 300g of fresh strawberries with 150g of caster sugar, the juice of 1 lemon and 200ml of water. Bring to the boil, then turn down and simmer for 15 minutes. Leave to cool for 1 hour. Mash the strawberries with the back of a spoon and strain through a fine sieve. Pour the cordial into a sterilised glass bottle and seal. Cool, then keep in the fridge for up to 2 weeks.*

# AMARO BANK BURST

Rich, refreshing, bittersweet

This cocktail is inspired by the immense power of an agitated river bursting its bank, as witnessed by bartender Marv Cunningham when Tropical Storm Karen hit Trinidad in 2019. A culinary cocktail that uses distinctive ingredients found in a kitchen, like spicy lemongrass and tamarind, which can also be used to delicious effect in a drink.

*Marv Cunningham, The Bahamas, Angostura Global Cocktail Competition winner, 2020*

### INGREDIENTS

- 30ml amaro di Angostura®
- 30ml Angostura® 1919 rum
- 150ml tamarind pulp
- 150ml spicy lemongrass syrup (see below)
- 30ml fresh coconut water
- 2 dashes of Angostura® orange bitters
- 5 dashes of Angostura® aromatic bitters

### GARNISH

* Lemongrass stalk and an edible flower

### GLASS

* Highball

### METHOD

1. Combine all the ingredients in a cocktail shaker.
2. Add some ice, then shake for around 15 seconds until well chilled.
3. Strain into a highball glass.
4. Add some ice to serve and garnish with a lemongrass stalk and an edible flower.

*Unusually, the modifying agent used here is tamarind pulp, which provides a rich acidic and tart backbone to the drink, while the spicy lemongrass syrup provides the sweet element. To make spicy lemongrass syrup, add a lemongrass stalk and a fresh red chilli to 120ml of water and 100g of sugar. Put over a low heat and stir until the sugar is all dissolved. Set aside and leave to cool for 1 hour. Strain into a sterilised glass bottle and seal. Refrigerate and use within a week.*

# CHEESEBOARD MANHATTAN

Bittersweet, fragrant and tangy

Is cheese served before or after dessert in your house? Either way, this cocktail complements your cheeseboard as perfectly as grapes and quince jam. It uses a British brandy, a grape-based spirit in place of whiskey, and a touch of quince jam for a sweet, floral twist on the classic Manhattan. The indulgent use of quince jam and the delicious edible garnish make this a fancy showstopper of a drink that will impress the most discerning of guests.

*Pritesh Mody, World of Zing*

### INGREDIENTS
- 50ml Burnt Faith brandy
- 1 tsp quince jam
- 10ml Cocchi rosso vermouth di Torino
- 10ml Cocchi extra dry vermouth di Torino
- 2 dashes of Angostura® aromatic bitters

### GARNISH
* A slice of Pecorino Toscano

### GLASS
* Coupe, chilled

### METHOD
1. Stir the brandy and quince jam together in a mixing glass until they have combined.
2. Add all the remaining ingredients and some ice and stir until chilled.
3. Fine strain into a chilled coupe glass.
4. Garnish with a slice of Pecorino Toscano.

> *Pecorino Toscano is a deliciously hard, salty, tangy cheese made from sheep's milk. An aged Spanish manchego is also made from sheep's milk and can be a suitable substitute.*

# AMARANTH

Elevated, nutty herbal

This is a twist on a Brandy Alexander, a dessert cocktail that was popular in the early twentieth century. This brandy classic is taken to new heights with two spirits, cognac and rum, as well as sherry, bitters and amaranth – a gluten free grain with a nutty, herbal slightly peppered taste.

*Recipe inspired by Krystian Kropaczewski, Artesian Bar London, 2023*

### INGREDIENTS
- 30ml Cognac
- 15ml Angostura 1824 aged rum
- 10ml oloroso sherry
- 20ml amaranth orgeat
- 2 dashes of Angostura® aromatic bitters
- 2 drops of saline solution
- 20ml double cream float

### GARNISH
* A chaff of amaranth grain and an edible flower

### GLASS
* Coupe

### METHOD
1. Add cognac, rum, sherry, amaranth orgeat to a mixing glass with ice.
2. Add the bitters and saline solution.
3. Stir for 15 seconds and strain into a coupe glass.
4. Float 20ml of double cream over the top.

---

*To make amaranth orgeat, blend 100g of amaranth grain into a fine flour and toast in a pan over a medium heat for around 10 minutes until dark brown, stirring constantly to avoid burning. Once cool, combine one part toasted flour with six parts water and strain the mixture through a cheesecloth. Add roughly 100g of sugar and stir over a low heat to make a syrup. Once cool, add two drops of orange blossom water. Store in a glass bottle in the refrigerator, will keep for up to a month.*

Angostura® bitters is a kitchen staple, and not just for cocktails. In Trinidad and Tobago, bitters is frequently used in food as well as drinks – from a few dashes in your morning coffee and fruit juice to rum punches and, of course, cocktails. Look closely at a bottle of bitters and you'll see suggestions for how to use it to impart exquisite flavour to a wide range of foods, from soups, salads and meat dishes to desserts.

Bitters can be enjoyed all the way through dinner and beyond. But, if you're unsure of how to get started, here are some simple pairing suggestions. Like in cocktails, bitters help bind flavours together. Orange bitters adds a citrusy depth of flavour to dishes, while the rich and nutty cocoa bitters is perfect for desserts. You'll often need more generous servings of bitters when adding it to food – regularly opting for spoonfuls versus dashes.

# PART 2

★

# SAVOURY

In the same way bitters adds a depth of flavour to iconic cocktails such as the Old Fashioned, it can also be used to enhance your favourite savoury dishes. It's the perfect secret ingredient – just a few dashes can elevate your dishes and delight your guests.

## SUMPTUOUS SOUPS

In the Caribbean, it's not unusual to add a teaspoon of Angostura® aromatic bitters to your broth. Like with an Old Fashioned, you may not initially notice the bitters, but you'll certainly notice its absence once you get used to it.

## ADDING DEPTH TO SAUCES

Even your standard tomato ketchup can be enhanced with a few dashes of bitters. For a winning finishing touch to a classic barbecue sauce, try adding a few dashes of Angostura® cocoa bitters as it adds an incredibly rich depth of flavour.

## SENSATIONAL SALADS

There are lots of ways to use bitters in salad dressings. Try adding it to enrich mayonnaise dressings with some fresh lemon juice and grated Parmesan cheese. Adding orange bitters to an olive oil-based dressing adds a zesty fragrance, while cocoa bitters can stand up well to the deeper flavours of balsamic-based dressings.

## FRAGRANT RICE

To add a zesty fragrance to coconut rice, cook 300g of white rice as per the packet instructions. Separately combine a knob of butter, 1 tablespoon of orange bitters, 1 tsp salt, ¼ teaspoon of nutmeg and a pinch of cayenne pepper. Stir this mixture into the cooked rice and then fold in 100g of shredded coconut, 35g of chopped spring onions and the zest of 1 orange.

## MAKE SEAFOOD SING

Orange bitters add a zesty, bright lift to fish dishes and 1 tablespoon of bitters works wonderfully in a lemon garlic marinade for prawns. All you need to do is combine 80ml of olive oil with the zest of 1 lemon, 1½ tablespoons of chopped fresh parsley, a couple of crushed cloves of crushed garlic, 1 teaspoon of salt and as much or as little chilli pepper as you can handle. At the end, add the 1 tablespoon of bitters to bind all those flavours together.

## UP YOUR CHILLI GAME

To elevate your chilli con carne, all it takes is 2 tablespoons of bitters. Cook off the onions and garlic, seal the meat and then add the bitters along with the other chilli ingredients. Bring to the boil, cover and simmer for 20 minutes, covered. Remove the lid and simmer for a final 30 minutes.

## MARINATING MEATS

Meat dishes in the Caribbean are always so succulent and flavoursome. The secret is often brining meat in a mixture of water, salt, sugar and spices before cooking. This serves to clean, moisturise and tenderise the meat and keep it fresh and juicy once cooked. After brining, it's then marinated. Caribbean cooking is big on flavour and the secret ingredient in a marinade is often a good few dashes of bitters.

## GLAZING HAM

For a sensational flavour twist on an easy, yet impressive, main dish, brush your joint of ham with a bitter honey glaze. Stir together 8 tablespoons of honey, 2 tablespoons of fresh lemon juice and 1 teaspoon of bitters, then glaze away!

# SWEET

In the book celebrating our centenary in 1924, there were a number of suggestions as to how to use bitters in desserts. While some of the recipes, such as blancmanges and cabinet puddings, have fallen out of fashion, others such as fruit salads, sponge cakes and ice cream are still perennial favourites and have stood the test of time – like bitters itself.

## FRUIT SALAD

Angostura® aromatic bitters works well in fruit juices and the same can be said for fruit salads. A few dashes add a subtle and delicate distinction that brings the natural fruit flavours to the fore.

## APPLE CRUMBLE

Bitters works well in apple-based cocktails, such as the Stone Fence (see page 32), so it stands to reason it adds the same richness and depth to the crispy topping of this traditional autumnal dessert. Add bitters to the butter, then combine with the flour, oats and sugar for an exceedingly good crumble topping.

## TRIFLE

Add a few dashes of bitters to the fruit jelly section of a trifle before setting and watch it boost the flavours with very little added effort.

## ADDING RICHNESS TO CHOCOLATE TREATS

Both cocoa and orange bitters enliven chocolate desserts, either with a nutty richness or a citrus lift.

## PASTRIES

Orange bitters has a magnificent yet delicate scent that livens up pastries. Add 1 teaspoon to your raw pastry dough mix and enjoy the enhanced aromas.

## A CLASSIC SPONGE MADE BETTER

Bitters is used in a classic sponge cake in our centenary book from 1924: 'Beat the yolks of 4 eggs until thick and creamy, add 2/3 cup of sugar, a little at a time, beating with an egg beater, add 3 tsp Angostura aromatic bitters, then the whites of the eggs, beaten until still. When the whites are partly mixed with the yolks and sugar, add 2/3 cup of sifted flour mixed with 1 tsp salt. Bake for 1 hour.'

## ICE CREAM TOPPING

Drizzle aromatic or orange bitters on top of ice cream. Or go one step further and make a bitters-rich chocolate sauce to drizzle over your ice cream. You can do this by combining 60ml of milk, 100g of cocoa powder, 2 teaspoons of Angostura® aromatic bitters and 2 teaspoons of brandy.

## PUMPKIN PIE

Add 2 teaspoons of orange bitters at the same time as the pumpkin to your pumpkin pie and just wait for your guests to ask what your secret ingredient is in the baked pie. It's a game changer.

## BEIGNETS

Add a generous quantity of cocoa bitters to your raw beignet dough and, once fried, you can finish these fluffy choux pastry balls with a dusting of icing sugar and more dashes of cocoa bitters for good measure.

# ACKNOWLEDGEMENTS

This is not the first time Angostura® has created a cocktail book. *Dr Siegert's Angostura Bitters*, published in 1906, includes 'recipes for mixing fancy drinks', many of which are today's classic cocktails. In 1924, 100 years ago, Angostura® published the *Giftbook of Cocktail and Other Recipes* to celebrate the brand's centenary. As a result, our latest cocktail book feels a little like picking up the baton and continuing the work of showcasing some of the incredible drinks made possible with Angostura®.

We would like to thank the employees of Angostura® for their unwavering dedication and continuous support. Their level of expertise has propelled the company to new heights, driving innovation and setting industry standards. With a deep understanding of the market and a commitment to excellence, they have successfully navigated challenges and seized opportunities, ensuring the company's sustained growth and success.

It is crucial to also thank the countless bartenders around the world who chose to develop recipes with Angostura® bitters over the past 200 years and to the many who took the time to document these recipes, which have been passed down over the past two centuries for generations to come. We would like to pay our respects to the late Gérard A. Besson, a historian who ensured so much of Angostura's rich history and fabled stories have been protected and documented for posterity.

A special thank you to all the bartenders who have entered the Angostura® Global Cocktail Challenges for the past 10 years and those currently using Angostura® bitters on menus today, who are helping to create and inspire more modern classic cocktails.

This cocktail book celebrates a historic 200 years of Angostura® bitters. Here's to another 200!

The House of Angostura

# INDEX

1

Published in 2024 by Ebury Press,
an imprint of Ebury Publishing
One Embassy Gardens, 8 Viaduct Gdns,
London SW11 7BW

Ebury Press is part of the Penguin Random House
group of companies whose addresses can be found at
global.penguinrandomhouse.com

First published by Ebury Press in 2024

www.penguin.co.uk

A CIP catalogue record for this book is available from
the British Library

ISBN 9781529938098

Design: Sandra Zellmer with Kasia Roy
Photography: Haarala Hamilton
Production: Percie Bridgwater
Project Editor: Fionn Hargreaves
Publishing Director: Elizabeth Bond
Drinks Stylist: Tom Woodward
Prop Stylist: Hannah Wilkinson
Angostura® Bitters Consultant: Vitra Deonarine
Angostura® Bitters Coordinator: Janeen Frection
Writer: Sarah Belizaire

Printed and bound in Germany by Mohn Media

The authorized representative in the EEA is Penguin
Random House Ireland, Morrison Chambers, 32
Nassau Street, Dublin, D02 YH68.

Penguin Random House is committed to a sustainable
future for our business, our readers and our planet.
This book is made from Forest Stewardship Council®
certified paper.